HOW TO FEEL BETTER

A HANDS-ON COMPANION FOR GETTING THROUGH TOUGH TIMES

TORI PRESS

A TARCHERPERIGEE BOOK

For
CLaIRE aND
Lucy

tarcherperigee

an imprint of Penguin Random House LLC

penguinrandomhouse.com

TarcherPerigee with tp colophon is a registered trademark of Penguin Random House LLC

Most TarcherPerigee books are available at special quantity discounts for bulk purchase for sales promotions, premiums, fund-raising, and educational needs. Special books or book excerpts also can be created to fit specific needs. For details, write: SpecialMarkets@penguinrandomhouse.com.

Hardcover ISBN: 9780593330401
eBook ISBN: 9780593330418

Printed in China

2 4 6 8 10 9 7 5 3 1

Book composition by Lorie Pagnozzi

SOMETIMES WE ALL FEEL BAD.

DESPAIR,
TURMOIL,
TOUGH TIMES,
DARK NIGHTS
OF THE SOUL:
aLL aRE aN INESCaPaBLE
PaRT OF LIFE aS a HuMaN.

I say "INESCAPABLE" BECAUSE, LIKE many PEOPLE, I HAVE TRIED — REALLY TRIED — To ESCAPE my BaD FEELINGS.

I'VE TRIED TO PREVENT THEM,

THEY CAN'T GHOST ME IF I GHOST THEM FIRST!

good VIBES ONLY To aVOID THEM,

To RESIST THEM,

I'm FINE

To NUMB THEM,

To PRETEND THEY DON'T EVEN EXIST.

REALLY, I'm FINE. I'm So ToTaLLY FINE.

BUT NO MATTER WHAT I DO, THEY STILL SHOW UP, RELENTLESS AND PERSISTENT, POWERFUL AND ALL-CONSUMING: A FORCE TO BE RECKONED WITH.

THERE IS NO ESCAPE FROM FEELING BAD.

BUT I'VE LEARNED
THERE ARE ways
OF FEELING
BETTER.

FEELING BETTER

ISN'T SOMETHING you CAN JUST DO. IT'S NOT INSTANT or automaTIC or EASY.

IT'S a PROCESS: SOMETHING you HAVE TO LEARN aND COMMIT TO aND PRACTICE. IT'S WORK.

THE WORK BEGINS WITH
FIGURING OUT YOUR
FEELINGS: LOOKING
INSIDE yourSELF, getting
To KNOW your VIBRANT
and CHANGING INNER
LANDSCAPE,

LEARNING To NOTICE and
RECOGNIZE and NAME
EVERYTHING you ENCOUNTER.

IT CONTINUES WITH SITTING WITH your FEELINGS: CULTIVATING PRACTICES THAT HELP you UNDERSTAND AND PROCESS your FEELINGS,

MAYBE EVEN OFFER yourself SUPPORT THROUGH THEM.

AND IT MIGHT NOT EVEN
BE WORK YOU CAN DO
ALL BY yourSELF,
WHICH IS WHY SOMETIMES
you NEED a LITTLE
EXTRa HELP

FROM a PROFESSIONAL.

DOING THE WORK OF
FEELING BETTER
IS NOT ALWAYS FUN.

IT'S OFTEN CONFRONTING
AND DAUNTING
AND ONEROUS
AND DEEPLY
UNCOMFORTABLE.
IT IS DIFFICULT WORK:
LIFE'S WORK.

BUT IT'S WORK THAT HOLDS THE PROMISE OF

EVER-EXPANDING
PEACE & FREEDOM

NOT BECAUSE IT
ELIMINATES
BAD FEELINGS or ENSURES
GOOD ONES,
BUT BECAUSE IT
CREATES SPACE
for ALL FEELINGS,

RELEASING you FROM THE
PRESSURE of NEEDING TO
FEEL GOOD
AND SETTING you FREE TO
FEEL BETTER.

THIS BOOK GREW FROM DARKNESS.

I WROTE IT FROM 2020-2021: THROUGH THE HEIGHT OF THE CORONAVIRUS PANDEMIC

THROUGH THE LOWS OF SOME OF THE DARKEST FEELINGS I'VE EVER EXPERIENCED

THROUGH MONTHS WHEN I STRUGGLED TO FEEL LIKE I COULD FUNCTION AT ALL.

I DID WHAT WORK I COULD—
aLONE aND IN THERapy—
To NaVIgaTE THE DaRKNESS.

I WORKED aT PRACTICES
THaT HaVE HELPED ME
FIND my way ouT oF
DaRKNESS BEFORE

I WORKED aLONG LINES oF
SELF-INQUIRY THaT
HaVE HELPED mE SEE
mySELF moRE CLEaRLy, caRE
FoR mySELF moRE INTENTIONaLLy
aND EVENTuaLLy, THaT woRK
BECamE THESE paGES.

THEY DO NOT CONTAIN EXPERT ADVICE, OR FOOLPROOF METHODS WITH guaranTEED RESULTS, OR

a magic FormuLa For FEELING BETTER ON DEMAND.

SOMETIMES THE ONLY THING you CAN DO IS STRUGGLE.

THAT'S OKAY.

THAT'S WHAT THIS BOOK
IS FOR.

IT'S a COMPANION FOR
THE TOUGH TIMES
THAT INEVITABLY
ARISE IN LIFE:

a PLACE To COME
FoR RESPITE AND
COMFoRT AND
COMPASSION,
IDEas & ENCouRagEMENT
To HELP You FIND youR
Way THRough THE DaRKNESS

AND IT'S ALSO a
SPRINGBOARD:
a JUMPING-OFF PLACE
TO INSPIRE you
TO FIND your OWN
ways of caring for
your own HEART,
WITH WRITING and DRAWING
EXERCISES INTENDED TO
HELP you ENCOUNTER and
UNDERSTAND your
FEELINGS IN NEW ways.

THIS BOOK HAS NO RULES TO FOLLOW.

IT OFFERS PLENTY OF WRITTEN EXERCISES, BUT you CAN CHOOSE HOW AND WHETHER TO COMPLETE THEM. IF AN EXERCISE FEELS LIKE TOO MUCH FOR NOW, you CAN ALWAYS PONDER IT WITHOUT WRITING ANYTHING, OR COME BACK TO IT LATER, OR SKIP IT ENTIRELY.

NOBODY'S HERE TO JUDGE. ♥

AND IF you maKE a MISTaKE IN PEN,

oR CAN'T BRINg yoursELF To WRITE IN a BOOK,

oR JUST WaNT a FEW EXTRa COPIES oF aN EXERCISE,

you CAN DOWNLOaD aLL oF THEm as PRINTaBLE PDFs aT REVELaToRi.com/FEELBETTER.

THERE IS NO RIGHT or WRONG WAY TO ENGAGE WITH THIS BOOK, so READ IT WITH a SENSE of OPENNESS aND CURIOSITY:

PERHaps NOT EVERY PRACTICE WILL RESONaTE WITH you

PERHaps NOT EVERY EXERCISE WILL REVEaL SoMETHINg (aT LEaST NoT IMMEDIaTELy)

BuT PERHaps you'LL FIND a NEW IDEa — EXPLoRE a NEW aVENUE — CoNSIDER a NEW PERSPECTIVE

AND PERHaps you'll FIND your OWN UNIQUE WAYS TO FEEL BETTER.

PART ONE
FIGURING OUT YOUR FEELINGS

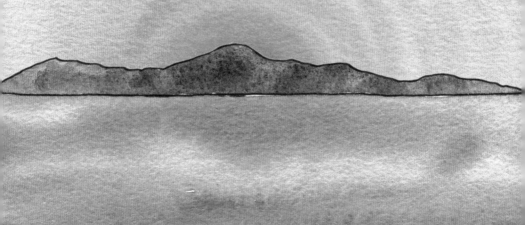

CHAPTER ONE

GET CURIOUS

TO PROPERLY COPE WITH AND MANAGE DIFFICULT FEELINGS YOU'LL NEED TO BE WILLING TO VENTURE INSIDE, TO OPEN UP YOUR HEART AND MIND, TO SEE EVERYTHING THAT DWELLS THERE: THINGS YOU MIGHT LIKE

AND THINGS YOU MIGHT NOT.

WHICH CAN BE a PRETTY SCARY THING. HERE BE MONSTERS

AND EVEN WHEN you CAN OVERCOME your FEAR— EVEN WHEN you're READY AND WILLING TO DO THE INNER WORK—

IT'S OFTEN HARD TO KNOW WHERE TO BEGIN. ♥

PRESS TO START

BUT THERE IS GOOD NEWS!

YOU DON'T HAVE TO DO ANYTHING TO BEGIN. YOU ARE ALREADY AT THE BEGINNING.

BECAUSE THE BEGINNING IS ALWAYS HERE AND NOW AND AT THE BEGINNING IS ALWAYS CURIOSITY:

A GENTLE, BENEVOLENT WONDER AT YOUR INNER LANDSCAPE.

CURIOSITY IS THE ABSENCE OF JUDGMENT: A MINDSET THAT DOES NOT LABEL THOUGHTS AND FEELINGS AS "GOOD" OR "BAD," A PERSPECTIVE THAT DOES NOT MAKE DEMANDS ABOUT WHAT SHOULD BE BUT INSTEAD GENTLY ASKS WHAT IS?

A CURIOUS MINDSET DOESN'T COME NATURALLY TO ME.

I'M MORE IN THE HABIT OF JUDGING AND LABELING

WHICH MAKES LOOKING INWARD MUCH MORE INTIMIDATING.

WHAT IF I FIND SOMETHING I DON'T LIKE? WHAT DO I DO?

IF I'M IN THE MINDSET OF JUDGMENT, I'LL DECIDE IT'S BAD. AND THEN I'LL FEEL WORSE:

OH NO! IT'S SOME-THING BAD! THIS IS REALLY BAD!

I'LL CREATE a SPIRAL OF FEELING BAD ABOUT FEELING BAD.

BUT IF I am IN a MINDSET OF
CURIOSITY...
EVERYTHING CHANGES.

I am NOT THERE to JUDGE.
I am an EXPLORER,
a TRAVELER:
TRAVERSING my INNER LANDSCAPE
TO SEE WHAT I FIND.
NOT TO PURSUE "GOOD" FEELINGS
or AVOID "BAD" ONES,
BUT SIMPLY TO LEARN
WHaT FEELINGS
are THERE.

GOOD
FEEL-
INGS

BAD
FEEL-
INGS

CURIOSITY IS NOT ALWAYS EASY TO CULTIVATE. BUT WITHOUT IT, WE CANNOT EVEN BEGIN.

HERE BE magic

SO THE VERY FIRST STEP IS TO EMBRACE WONDER OVER JUDGMENT — TO SET ASIDE LABELS AND SIMPLY BE CURIOUS ABOUT YOUR VARIED, COMPLEX, TUMULTUOUS, HUMAN FEELINGS

SO THEY MAY SPEAK THEIR MESSAGES AND SHARE WITH YOU THEIR WISDOM.

THINK aBout a TIME you
JUDGED SomETHING or
SoMEONE... THEN LEaRNED
a NEW DETaIL THaT maDE you
CHaNGE your mIND. HOW DID
IT FEEL? _____

_____
_____
_____
_____
_____
_____
_____

DID your INITIaL JuDGMENT HaVE
aNy REPERCuSSIONS? _____

_____
_____
_____
_____
_____

WHAT MIGHT HAVE BEEN
DIFFERENT IF YOU'D BEEN
CURIOUS INSTEAD OF
JUDGMENTAL IN THE BEGINNING?

_____
_____
_____
_____
_____
_____
_____
_____
_____
_____

HOW MIGHT YOU HAVE FELT
DIFFERENTLY? _____
_____
_____
_____
_____

GET SOME PRACTICE
PRACTICING CURIOSITY ♥

JOT DOWN a FEW
THINGS you TEND
To BE JUDGY aBOUT:

_____
_____
_____
_____
_____
_____
_____
_____
_____
_____
_____
_____
_____
_____
_____

BRAINSTORM SOME
WAYS you CAN BE
CURIOUS INSTEAD:

_____
_____
_____
_____
_____
_____
_____
_____
_____
_____
_____
_____
_____
_____
_____

IT'S OKAY!
WE ALL
HAVE SOME!

GREAT
IDEAS!

WAYS TO PRACTICE CURIOSITY

THINK OF YOUR EMOTIONS AS MESSENGERS.

THEY HAVE SOMETHING TO TELL YOU, IF YOU'RE LISTENING.

SADNESS

GIVE YOURSELF SPACE. ACKNOWLEDGE YOUR LOSS.

ANGER

MAYBE IT'S TIME TO SET a BOUNDARY.

YOU ARE IN THE PRESENCE OF SOMETHING WONDERFUL AND WORTH KEEPING.

JOY

RESIST THE URGE TO LABEL.

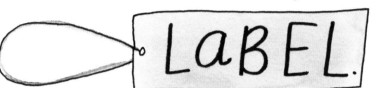

PUTTING LABELS ON EMOTIONS CAN TURN THEM INTO EITHER **FRIENDS** OR **FOES.** BUT THEY ARE NEITHER: THEY ARE MESSENGERS. THEY ARE INFORMATION. SOME ARE MORE PLEASANT TO EXPERIENCE THAN OTHERS, BUT ALL HAVE A PURPOSE IN YOUR LIFE.

ASK QUESTIONS.

ENGAGE WITH YOUR EMOTIONS BY ASKING THEM CURIOSITY QUESTIONS.

WHY ARE YOU HERE?

WHAT BROUGHT YOU OUT?

WTF IS YOUR DEAL?! ← (THEY DON'T HAVE TO BE POLITE QUESTIONS.)

YOU MIGHT NOT GET ANY ANSWERS, OR ANY SATISFYING ONES. THAT'S OKAY.

IT'S NOT ABOUT THE ANSWERS. (MAYBE THERE AREN'T ANY ANSWERS.)

WHAT ARE YOU TRYING TO TELL ME?

IT'S ABOUT BEING WILLING TO ASK.

SEPARATE YOURSELF FROM YOUR FEELINGS.

SOMETIMES I FEEL LIKE I MERGE WITH MY FEELINGS: LIKE THEY ARE SO BIG AND INTENSE THAT **I BECOME** THEM.

I EVEN TALK ABOUT MY FEELINGS THIS WAY:

I am aNGRY

INSTEAD OF

I FEEL aNgry

BUT I am NOT WHAT I FEEL. NOR aRE you.

I am NOT my EMOTIONS. I am THE OBSERVER OF my EMOTIONS. I am THE one NAVIGATING my JOURNEY. I am THE LEADER. I am THE WITNESS. I am THE SUBJECT and THE STUDENT and THE TEACHER.

AND I CAN ALWAYS REMEMBER THIS BY RETURNING TO MY STARTING PLACE OF CURIOSITY.

WHAT are SoME FEELINGS
you WISH you NEVER HaD
To FEEL again?_____
_____
_____
_____
_____
_____

WHAT are SoME
FEELINGS you
JUDGE yourSELF For HaVING?
_____
_____
_____
_____
_____
_____
_____
_____

NOW, THINK ABOUT HOW you
MIGHT APPROACH THE FEELINGS
you JUST WROTE ABOUT WITH A
MINDSET OF CURIOSITY. WHAT
QUESTIONS COULD you ask THEM?

_____
_____
_____
_____
_____
_____
_____

HOW DO you THINK THEY
     MIGHT RESPOND?

_____
_____
_____
_____
_____
_____

TELL SOME OF YOUR FEELINGS EXACTLY HOW YOU FEEL ABOUT THEM (DON'T HOLD BACK!)

ANXIETY

SADNESS

FEAR

SHAME

NOW, IMAGINE WHAT YOUR FEELINGS MIGHT BE TRYING TO TELL YOU:

ANXIETY

SADNESS

FEAR

SHAME

CHAPTER TWO

PRACTICE MINDFULNESS

WHAT IS MINDFULNESS AND WHAT DOES IT HAVE TO DO WITH FEELING BETTER?

IT'S A POPULAR BUZZWORD, TOSSED AROUND IN CONVERSATIONS ABOUT GROWTH AND SPIRITUALITY AND MENTAL HEALTH.

TO ME, IT ALWAYS SOUNDED INTIMIDATING.

a MYSTICAL, MAGICAL STATE,
DIFFICULT TO ATTAIN,
ACCESSIBLE ONLY TO SAGES
AND ASCETICS AND GURUS.
(AND I AM ANYTHING BUT A guru.)

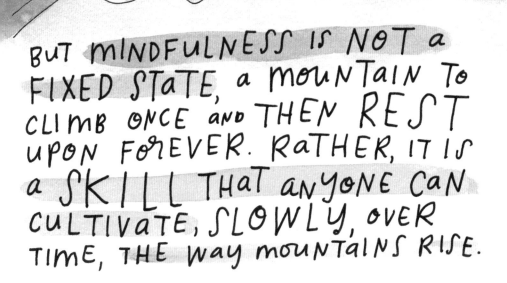

BUT MINDFULNESS IS NOT A
FIXED STATE, A MOUNTAIN TO
CLIMB ONCE AND THEN REST
UPON FOREVER. RATHER, IT IS
A SKILL THAT ANYONE CAN
CULTIVATE, SLOWLY, OVER
TIME, THE WAY MOUNTAINS RISE.

BEING MINDFUL REALLY MEANS
BEING aware:
USING your SENSES.
Paying aTTENTioN.
TUNING IN.
NOTICING.
allowing WHATEVER
IS HAPPENING
To HAPPEN,

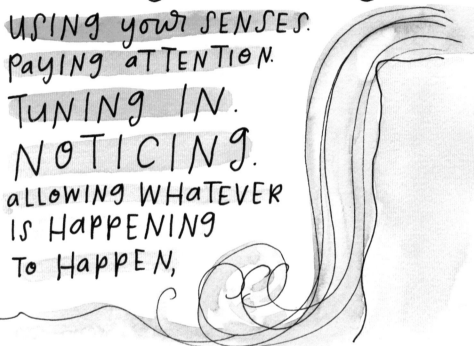

WITHOUT TRYING TO
ENgage or INTERFERE
WITH IT.

MINDFULNESS IS a PRESENCE IN THE PRESENT.

I'VE FOUND THE MOST EFFECTIVE WAY TO PRACTICE MINDFULNESS IS

MEDITATION.

MEDITATION IS a FORMAL PRACTICE: a WAY OF DELIBERATELY CREATING SPACE AND TIME TO STRENGTHEN YOUR POWERS OF OBSERVATION AND AWARENESS.

AND IT CAN TAKE MANY FORMS, NOT JUST THIS ONE!

IN MEDITATION, you PRACTICE MINDFULNESS BY FOCUSING your FULL aTTENTION ON a SPECIFIC OBJECT:

SOMETHING OTHER THAN THE ENDLESS STREAM OF THINKING aND SELF-TaLK THaT USUaLLY CROWDS your BRaIN (WHETHER you NOTICE IT OR NOT).

I REALLY SHOULD...
WHAT IF I...?
DID I REMEMBER TO..

THE OBJECT OF FOCUS CaN BE aLMOST aNYTHING:

a SOUND

a SENSaTION

EVEN a SMELL.

BUT TRADITIONALLY, FOCUS IS ON THE BREATH.

WE BREaTHE
auTomaTicaLLy,
WITHOUT THOUGHT
OR INTENTION,
OUR BODIES DOING
THE WORK OF KEEPING US
ALIVE AND OXYGENaTED
EVEN as OUR MINDS ENGAGE
IN DRIFTING AND WORRYING
AND TELLING US STORIES.

BUT IN MEDITATION,
YOU BRING THIS
auTomaTic
AND MINDLESS
PROCESS TO THE
FOREFRONT OF
YOUR awaRENESS.

You MIGHT FEEL THE COOLNESS OF THE BREATH as IT ENTERS THE NOSTRILS, or THE EXPANSION of THE CHEST as THE LUNGS FILL, or THE FRESH OXYGEN TRAVELING THROUGH THE BLOODSTREAM To NOURISH your organs. You MIGHT SENSE THE WARMTH OF THE BREATH as IT EXITS THE BODY, THE GENTLE CONTRACTION OF THE BELLY AND LUNGS as THEY PUSH IT BACK OUT.

REST your aTTENTION ON ANY OF THESE SENSaTIONS CREaTED BY THE BREaTH.

So SIMPLE. So EaSY.

AND YET NOT SIMPLE or EaSY aT aLL.

INEVITaBLY, THOUGHTS WILL CREEP IN AND STEAL THE FOCUS OF your aTTENTION FROM THE BREaTH.

You CaN'T STOP THIS FROM HaPPENING. (NOR SHOULD you TRY TO.)

You PROBaBLY WON'T EVEN REaLIZE IT'S HaPPENED aT FIRST.

BREaTHING IN... BREaTHING OUT...
BREaTHING IN... BRE — IS
THaT mY DOG BaRKING?
OH NO, IS HE DISTURBING
THE NEIGHBORS? THaT
REMINDS ME, I NEED TO...

BUT THE MOMENT YOU DO NOTICE IS THE magic MOMENT OF AWARENESS.

I'M SO BEHIND ON MY TO-DO LIST, WHEN WILL I FIND TIME TO — WAIT! I'M THINKING! OK — BREATHING IN... BREATHING OUT...

THE MOMENT YOU NOTICE AND OBSERVE YOUR THOUGHTS IS THE VERY MOMENT YOU CAN FREE YOURSELF FROM THEM, CHOOSING INSTEAD TO LET THEM DISSIPATE AS YOU RETURN TO THE BREATH.

IN THIS MOMENT, YOU ARE PRACTICING MINDFULNESS.

You can mark THIS INSTANT USING THE TECHNIQUE of NOTING: naming THE THOUGHT as you NOTICE IT, THEN RELEASING IT.

I usually use a SINGLE WORD To NOTE: "THINKING" or "PLANNING" or "WORRYING" or "REGRETTING." BuT aNYTHING CAN BE a NOTE: a WORD, a PHRASE, EVEN a MENTAL ImagE. THE IDEa IS To NOTICE aND NAME WHaT COMES INTO your mINd So THaT you CaN CONSCIOUSLY LET IT go.

SPEND a FEW SECONDS
IN MEDITaTION RIGHT NOW.
FOLLOW THE LINE FROM STaRT
To FINISH, WITHOUT LETTING
YOUR EYES STRaY:

NOW
TaKE
a FuLL,
DEEP
BREaTH

HOW DIFFICULT WAS IT NOT TO LET
your VISION WANDER? WERE you
SURPRISED? WERE you DISTRACTED
BY ANYTHING, LIKE THE TEXT at
THE CENTER OF THE SPIRAL?

_____

_____

_____

_____

_____

DO you FEEL ANY DIFFERENT
AFTER DOING THIS EXERCISE?
WRITE WHAT you NOTICE HERE:

_____

_____

_____

_____

_____

_____

_____

_____

_____

_____

LOOK FORWARD TO DISTRACTIONS

WHEN I FIRST STARTED TO MEDITATE, I TRIED TO WIN AT IT.

I SET goALS* FOR MySELF:

BEST MEDITATOR EVER

*ONLY ONE OF THESE gOALS IS ACTUALLY ACHIEVABLE.

☐ MEDITATE EVERY SINGLE DAY

☐ ACHIEVE a PERFECTLY PEACEFUL MIND

☐ ALWAYS STAY FOCUSED ON EVERY BREATH

☐ NEVER GET DISTRACTED

BUT WHEN I SaT DOWN TO MEDITaTE, I FOUND THAT I OFTEN COULD NOT EVEN maKE IT THROUGH a SINGLE BREATH WITHOUT GETTING SIDETRaCKED BY mY TRAIN OF THOUGHT.

AND WORSE, EVERY TIME I NOTICED mY mIND WANDERING, I WOULD JumP IN WITH JUDGMENTS AND NEGaTIVE SELF-TaLK.

omg! STaY FOCUSED! YOU aRE FaILING aT THIS! HOW HaRD IS IT TO NOTICE YOUR BREaTH?

(PRETTY HaRD, IT TURNS OUT)

I WaS TURNING mY PRaCTICE INTO a PLACE OF JUDGMENT— a PLACE I DREaDED GOING.

I HAD TO LEARN TO **LOOK FORWARD TO DISTRACTIONS.**

DISTRACTIONS ARE **ESSENTIAL** TO YOUR PRACTICE BECAUSE THEY **HELP IT GROW.**

EVERY TIME YOU BECOME DISTRACTED AND HAVE TO REFOCUS YOUR aTTENTION ON THE BREaTH, YOU aRE TRaINING YOUR MIND To EXTRICaTE ITSELF FROM ITS OWN CONSTaNT BaRRaGE OF THOUGHTS. YOU aRE aWaKENING, LITTLE BY LITTLE, To YOUR TRUE NaTUrE: LEarNING TO RISE aBOVE THE WINDS OF THOUGHT & FEELING

aND SEE YOUrSELF as YOU REaLLY arE.

SO **LOOK FORWARD** TO **DISTRACTIONS** IN YOUR MEDITATION PRACTICE.

WELCOME THEM WHEN THEY ARRIVE. OPEN THE DOOR TO THEM AND GREET THEM WITH JOY. MAYBE EVEN THANK THEM FOR GIVING YOU THE GREAT OPPORTUNITY TO EXPERIENCE THE MOMENT OF MINDFULNESS.

CAUGHT MY MIND WANDERING ♥

a map of WHERE DURING ME

RANDOMLAND
- A GRAB BAG OF WEIRDNESS
- I WONDER WHAT IT FEELS LIKE TO HAVE RABIES?

THE ANCIENT PAST
- RELIVE OLD ARGUMENTS AND EMBARRASSMENTS!
- DWELL ON STUFF THAT CAN'T BE CHANGED!

· NOTICE THE THOUGHT ·

THE SHADOW
- NEGATIVE SELF-TALK
- JUDGMENT AND SELF-CRITICISM
- ALL MY WORST THOUGHTS

THE IDEA FACTORY
"I JUST HAD A GREAT IDEA! BETTER STOP MEDITATING & JOT IT DOWN!"

MY MIND WANDERS
DITATION

CATCH THE MIND
WANDERING

THE MENTAL
TO-DO LIST

HOME ♥

THE BREATH

To Do

- ALL 80,506 THINGS I NEED TO DO THAT I ONLY EVER REMEMBER WHEN I'M MEDITATING
- GROCERIES TO BUY, ERRANDS TO RUN,

A SENSE THAT IT ALL HAS TO HAPPEN URGENTLY AND THIS MEDITATION IS WASTING MY TIME

REMEMBER THE BREATH

THE FUTURE

- WORRY! ANXIETY! FRETTING!
- WHAT-IFS AND CATASTROPHIZING
- EXCITEMENT AND ANTICIPATION
- WHATS FOR DINNER?

SPEND a FEW MINUTES IN
MEDITATION. DON'T TRY TO STOP
your MIND FROM WANDERING—
JUST NOTICE WHERE IT GOES,
and CREATE your OWN MAP.

HOME
THE
BREATH

WHaT DID your mIND LOOK
LIKE DURING YOUR MEDITATION?
DRaW (OR DOODLE OR SCRIBBLE)
IT BELOW:

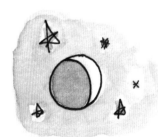

MINDFULNESS GOES WHEREVER You DO

Your MINDFULNESS PRACTICE DOESN'T always HAVE To TAKE PLACE IN a FORMAL SETTING.

You CAN TAP INTO IT WHEREVER you are!

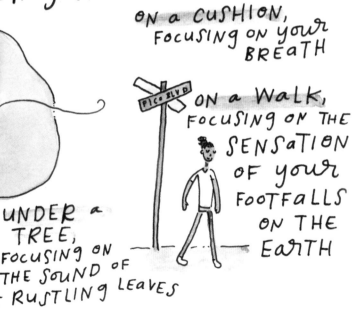

ON a CUSHION, FOCUSING ON your BREATH

ON a WALK, FOCUSING ON THE SENSATION OF your FOOTFALLS ON THE EARTH

UNDER a TREE, FOCUSING ON THE SOUND OF RUSTLING LEAVES

FOLDING THE LAUNDRY,

FOCUSING ON THE FEEL OF FABRIC against your FINGERTIPS, SENDING LOVING KINDNESS TO THE OWNER OF EACH garment (ESPECIALLY IF IT'S YOU!)

SITTING IN TRAFFIC,

FOCUSING ON THE RISE and FALL of your HEART RATE as you NAVIGATE your commute and INTERACT WITH OTHER DRIVERS

WHEN YOU CAN'T SLEEP,

FOCUSING ON your muscLES as you RELAX THEM, ONE BY ONE, FROM HEAD TO TOE

CARING FOR a PET or a PLANT,

FOCUSING ON THEIR ENERGY, THEIR LIVING VITALITY, THEIR RESPONSE TO your LOVING ATTENTION

CHOOSE a MUNDANE ACTIVITY — LIKE
SWEEPING THE FLOOR, OR WASHING
THE DISHES, OR TAKING a SHOWER—
AND DO IT AS MINDFULLY AS you
CAN. REALLY PAY ATTENTION TO
ALL OF THE SENSATIONS you
EXPERIENCE. HOW DID IT FEEL?

_____

_____

_____

_____

_____

_____

WAS IT EASY OR HARD TO FOCUS?
DID you FIND yourSELF OPERATING
ON AUTOPILOT AT ANY POINT?

_____

_____

_____

_____

_____

_____

EVERY SECOND COUNTS 🕐

You DON'T HAVE TO MEDITATE FOR 4 HOURS a DAY TO SEE BENEFITS. You DON'T HAVE TO MAKE a BIG TIME COMMITMENT AT ALL, IN FACT.

TEN SECONDS OF BREATH AWARENESS IS a WIN. 💜

FULLY EXPERIENCING HALF a BREATH IS AN ACCOMPLISHMENT.

ANY TIME, HOWEVER SHORT, you SPEND IN MINDFULNESS IS TIME you ARE DOING THE WORK.

THE WORK OF MINDFULNESS IS CUMULATIVE.

AT FIRST, IT CAN BE HARD TO SEE. THE PAYOFFS ARE SMALL AND SUBTLE: A MOMENT OF AWARENESS AS YOU DRINK YOUR MORNING COFFEE (MAYBE YOU ENJOY THE FLAVOR A LITTLE MORE, TOO)...

A BRIEF PAUSE IN YOUR MENTAL DIALOGUE AS YOU GO ABOUT YOUR DAY (MAYBE A NEW RECOGNITION OF THE DIALOGUE ITSELF)...

THE DISCOVERY OF AN EMOTION AS IT RISES WITHIN YOU, BEFORE IT OVERWHELMS YOUR CONSCIOUSNESS.

LITTLE BY LITTLE, THESE MOMENTS BUILD ON ONE ANOTHER. THEY MAY HAPPEN MORE OFTEN AS YOU CONTINUE TO PRACTICE, SLOW AND STEADFAST, CREATING A FOUNDATION OF AWARENESS,

ENABLING YOU TO SEE YOURSELF AS SEPARATE FROM YOUR EMOTIONS AND TO FEEL MORE CAPABLE OF COPING WITH THEM.

A REGULAR MINDFULNESS PRACTICE IS a LITTLE LIKE MAGIC. IT BRINGS a MEASURE OF CALM AND EASE TO DAILY LIFE. IT OFFERS a PATHWAY TO a DEEPER UNDERSTANDING OF your JOYS— your STRUGGLES— YOURSELF.

MEDITATION LOG

TODAY IN MEDITATION I FELT:

- [ ] JITTERY
- [ ] DIALED-IN
- [ ] EXCITED
- [ ] MELLOW
- [ ] DISTRACTED
- [ ] BUSY
- [ ] BORED
- [ ] CURIOUS
- [ ] _____
- [ ] _____

- [ ] THOUGHTFUL
- [ ] HIGH-STRUNG
- [ ] CHECKED OUT
- [ ] JUDGMENTAL
- [ ] THOUGHT FULL
- [ ] OFF-KILTER
- [ ] MELANCHOLY
- [ ] HALFHEARTED
- [ ] _____
- [ ] _____

MY MIND SPENT TIME IN a
_____ PLACE AND a
_____ PLACE.

I MEDITATED FOR _____
(SECONDS/MINUTES/HOURS)...
AND THEY ALL COUNT!

CHAPTER THREE

DEEPEN your AWARENESS

I usually THINK aBouT my EMOTIONAL STATE IN PRETTY BaSIC LaNguaGe:

Happy   SaD

ANgRY   AFRaID

BUT THESE WORDS RARELY CAPTURE THE FULL AND BRILLIANT SCOPE OF MY EMOTIONAL UPS AND DOWNS...

SO I'VE FOUND IT HELPFUL TO PINPOINT MY EMOTIONS BY NAMING THEM ACCURATELY.

SEETHING ISN'T THE SAME AS PERTURBED.

EBULLIENT IS VERY DIFFERENT FROM GLAD.

BUMMED IS WORLDS APART FROM MISERABLE.

GIVING MY FEELINGS SPECIFIC NAMES HELPS ME GRAPPLE WITH THEM A LITTLE MORE EFFECTIVELY. IT'S EMPOWERING TO KNOW EXACTLY WHAT I'm DEALING WITH.

IF THESE WATERCOLORS
REPRESENTED SOME OF YOUR
EMOTIONS, WHAT WOULD THEY BE?
GIVE THEM NAMES (AND FACES TOO,
IF YOU LIKE.)

BOOST your EmOTIONAL VOCABULARY

CULTIVaTE EMOTIONAL awareNESS BY GETTING FamiLiar WITH THE FULL SPECTRUM OF your FEELINGS.

ON THE FOLLOWING PAGES, THINK aBOUT ALL OF THE EMOTIONAL NUANCE CONVEYED BY EACH NAMED FEELING—AND FILL IN SOME NAMES OF your OWN!

are you FEELING
ANGRY? or...
HOSTILE MAD
AGITATED TENSE
SALTY FRUSTRATED
ON EDGE RESENTFUL
BITTER IRATE
EXASPERATED DEF-ENSIVE
VINDICTIVE (FILL IN YOUR OWN)

_____   _____
_____   _____
_____   _____
_____   _____

SaD? or... 🌸

INDIFFERENT gloomy
DOWN-
CAST HURT
DESPAIRING NUMB
BLEAK
LISTLESS MOROSE
WRETCHED DIS-
couraged
WITH-
DRAWN APATHETIC
DISAPPOINTED CRUSHED

_____   _____
_____   _____
_____

Happy?

or...

SATISFIED FREE

CONFIDENT

INSPIRED VINDI-CATED

glaD EXPANSIVE

BLISSFUL ELATED

FULFILLED PEACEFUL

PLEaSED ENTHUSIASTIC

calm

_____   _____

_____   _____

_____   _____

FEARFUL? or...

alarmed anxious
overwhelmed JITTERY
SKITTISH
apprehensive HIGH-STRUNG

_____

SURPRISED? or...

BEWILDERED SHOOK
HESITANT STARTLED
DUMBFOUNDED aghast
TAKEN aBACK THUNDERSTRUCK

_____

DISGUSTED? or...

REPULSED JADED
ASHAMED UNCOMFORTABLE
UNEASY DISTURBED

_____ _____
_____ _____

STRESSED? or...

HARRIED PESSIMISTIC
HELPLESS NERVOUS
WOUND-UP
OUT OF CONTROL UPSET

_____ _____
_____ _____

CHOOSE 3 OF THE EMOTIONS NAMED IN THE LAST 5 PAGES AND THINK ABOUT HOW THEY FEEL. WHEN HAVE YOU ENCOUNTERED THEM, AND WHAT DIFFERENTIATES THEM FROM OTHER, SIMILAR FEELINGS?

① _____

_____

_____

_____

_____

_____

_____

_____

_____

_____

_____

_____

_____

_____

②

③

TRY a BODY SCAN MEDITATION

SOMETIMES THE BODY GIVES you IMPORTANT CLUES aBOUT HOW you FEEL. IT may EVEN RECOGNIZE and RESPOND TO your EMOTIONS BEFORE you DO. (EVER HOLD your BREATH WITHOUT NOTICING?)

maybE IN mEDITaTION you've OBSERVED THaT your BREaTH cHanGES aLONG WITH your EMOTIONaL STaTE.

STRESS ← → CaLm

RaPID, SHaLLOW BREaTHING   SLOW, DEEP BREaTHING

A FULL-BODY SCAN MIGHT REVEAL EVEN MORE.

STARTING AT THE TOP OF YOUR HEAD, REST YOUR ATTENTION FOR A FEW MOMENTS ON EACH PART OF YOUR BODY, FROM TOP TO BOTTOM.

NOTICE HOW EVERY PART FEELS. MAYBE YOU CAN FEEL YOUR PULSE, OR WARMTH, OR COOLNESS, OR A SENSATION LIKE TINGLING OR BUZZING.

LOOK OUT FOR PLACES THAT ARE HOLDING TENSION OR DISCOMFORT. CHECK IN ON OBVIOUS SPOTS, LIKE THE SHOULDERS, AND ALSO SMALLER, MORE OVERLOOKED AREAS, LIKE THE SPACE BETWEEN YOUR JAW AND YOUR EAR.

WHEN YOU ENCOUNTER TENSION OR DISCOMFORT, DON'T IMMEDIATELY MOVE TO RESIST, CHANGE, OR FIX IT. JUST ACKNOWLEDGE IT. MAYBE EVEN THANK IT BEFORE MOVING ON: YOUR BODY IS SENDING A MESSAGE ABOUT HOW YOU'RE FEELING.

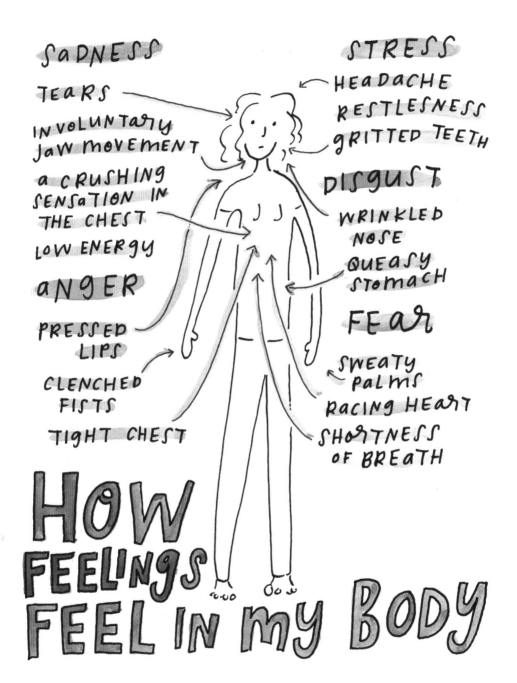

SADNESS

TEARS

INVOLUNTARY JAW MOVEMENT

A CRUSHING SENSATION IN THE CHEST

LOW ENERGY

ANGER

PRESSED LIPS

CLENCHED FISTS

TIGHT CHEST

STRESS

HEADACHE
RESTLESNESS
GRITTED TEETH

DISGUST

WRINKLED NOSE

QUEASY STOMACH

FEAR

SWEATY PALMS

RACING HEART

SHORTNESS OF BREATH

HOW FEELINGS FEEL IN MY BODY

WHERE DO your FEELINGS SHOW UP IN your BODY?

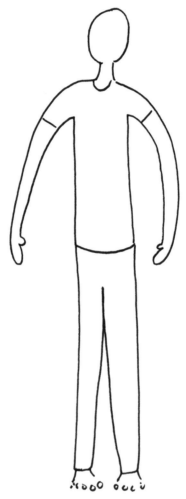

LABEL, DRAW, OR COLOR THEM IN.

PART TWO

SITTING WITH your FEELINGS

CHAPTER FOUR

REMEMBER your FEELINGS are TEMPORARY

ALMOST* all FEELINGS are Temporary VISITORS.

THEY DON'T FEEL THAT WAY, THOUGH.
WHEN I'M OVERWHELMED BY MY
EMOTIONS,
I'm always sure
THEY'LL LAST
FOREVER...

I'LL NEVER BE Happy again.

* UNWANTED FEELINGS THAT LINGER TOO LONG MAY CALL FOR A LITTLE EXTRA HELP: SEE PART 3 ♥

BUT THEY DON'T.
THEY JUST DON'T.
LIKE THE moon
AND THE WEATHER,
LIKE our HUMAN SELVES,
THEY are DYNAMIC.
THEY SHIFT.
THEY CHANGE.

EVEN THE STRONGEST, WILDEST, MOST PERSISTENT FEELINGS are ONLY PASSING THROUGH, SOON TO BE REPLACED BY SOMETHING NEW.

AND SOMETIMES, REMEMBERING my FEELINGS are TEMPORARY makes RIDING THEM OUT a LITTLE BIT EaSIER.

THERE are many ways to REMIND yourself of THE TRANSIENT and EPHEMERAL nature of your FEELINGS, so get curious—EXPLORE AND FIND your OWN PERSONAL PRACTICE.

HERE are a FEW THAT HAVE HELPED ME:

GIVE YOURSELF A CHANGE OF SCENERY

SOMETIMES WHEN you CAN'T CHANGE HOW you FEEL, IT CAN HELP To **CHANGE SOMETHING ELSE** — To PAUSE AND DO SOMETHING DIFFERENT, JUST FOR a SHORT WHILE.

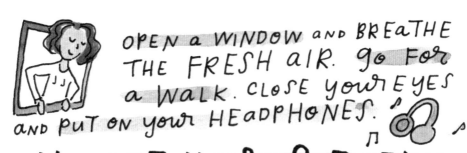

OPEN a WINDOW AND BREATHE THE FRESH AIR. Go FOR a WALK. CLOSE your EYES AND PUT ON your HEADPHONES.

CHANGE your SCENERY.

I DON'T MEAN THIS AS GLIB ADVICE — AS THOUGH ALL YOU NEED TO DO TO ASSUAGE YOUR GRIEF OR BANISH YOUR DEPRESSION IS GET SOME SUNSHINE.

A CHANGE OF SCENERY IS NOT AN ATTEMPT TO MAKE UNWANTED FEELINGS VANISH.

IT'S A WAY TO HELP YOURSELF SEE BEYOND YOUR CURRENT CIRCUMSTANCES,

TO REMIND YOURSELF YOU ARE NOT TRAPPED IN ANY ONE PLACE, OR IN ANY ONE FEELING.

A CHANGE OF SCENERY IS a WAY OF PUTTING YOURSELF IN THE PATH OF THE NEW, THE DIFFERENT, THE UNEXPECTED.

MAYBE THE TOUCH OF SUNLIGHT ON your FACE WILL REMIND YOU THAT WARMTH AND JOY ARE REAL, THAT THEY PERSIST EVEN WHEN THEY SEEM TO HAVE GONE...

MAYBE WATCHING AN INSECT WINGING ITS RANDOM WAY ALONG WILL REMIND YOU THAT YOURS IS NOT THE ONLY PATH THAT SOMETIMES SEEMS CROOKED AND MEANDERING.

MAYBE GAZING OUT A RAINY WINDOW WILL REMIND YOU OF THE MANY WAYS THE WORLD HAS OF CLEANSING AND RENEWING ITSELF.

AND MAYBE A MOMENTARY FLASH OF A NEW OR DIFFERENT FEELING, AN UNEXPECTED ENCOUNTER, WILL REMIND YOU THAT ALL FEELINGS ARE TEMPORARY.

COME BACK TO THIS PAGE THE
NEXT TIME YOU ARE FEELING a
STRONG EMOTION.
WHAT DO YOU FEEL?
_____

HOW DOES IT FEEL? _____
_____
_____
_____
_____
_____
_____

NOW, go ON a 10-MINUTE WALK or
OTHERWISE GIVE YOURSELF a CHANGE
OF SCENERY. HOW DO YOU FEEL NOW?
_____
_____
_____
_____
_____
_____

DO YOU STILL FEEL THE SAME STRONG
EMOTION? ARE YOU EXPERIENCING IT
IN THE SAME WAY? HAVE ANY OTHER
FEELINGS COME UP? _____

_____
_____
_____
_____
_____
_____
_____
_____
_____

RETURN TO THIS PAGE AFTER 24
HOURS HAVE PASSED. HOW DO
YOU FEEL NOW? _____

_____
_____
_____
_____
_____

CONNECT WITH SOMETHING Larger THan yourSELF

CHANGING your SCENERY ISN'T THE ONLY way To GET a NEW PERSPECTIVE. SOMETIMES IT ALSO HELPS To CONNECT WITH SOMETHING Larger THan yourSELF, SOMETHING THAT HELPS you REMEMBER HOW COMMON

AND ORDINARY IT IS FOR HUMAN
BEINGS TO STRUGGLE.

YOU CAN FIND THIS CONNECTION
IN MANY PLACES:
a YOGA STUDIO, a HOUSE OF
WORSHIP, a PHONE CALL
WITH a FRIEND.

ONCE I FOUND IT aT
THE BEACH.
I WAS GOING THROUGH
a PARTICULARLY DARK TIME,
AND AT THE END OF a SESSION,
MY THERAPIST SAID:
"GO TO THE BEACH
SOMETIME THIS WEEK."

LIKE a LOT OF PEOPLE IN L.A.,
I LIVE WITHIN DRIVING DISTANCE
OF SEVERAL BEAUTIFUL BEACHES
THAT I almOST NEVER VISIT.

BUT I PROMISED my
  THERAPIST I WOULD go.

THAT WEEKEND, I PACKED a
SmaLL Bag anD DROVE INTO
SaNTa MONICa. I PICKED a
SPOT NEaR THE WaTER anD
DUg my TOES INTO THE SaND.

I BREATHED.

I WATCHED AS THE
WAVES ROSE AND FELL:
RELENTLESS, AUTOMATIC,
UNSTOPPABLE.
LIKE MY BREATH.

I FELT THE SUN ON MY SKIN
AND THE EARTH, TINY BROKEN
GRAINS OF ANCIENT ROCK,
BENEATH MY BARE FEET.

I FELT THE RHYTHM OF THE
WAVES IN MY BODY: ONE
VESSEL OF LIVING WATER
RESPONDING TO ANOTHER.

IN a PRIMAL way, FoR
JUST a momENT, I
FELT CONNECTED To
EVERY OTHER HumaN
WHO, OVER mILLENNIa,
HaD EVER SaT IN QUIET
CONTEMPLaTION OF THE
EaRTH aND SEa aND SKY.

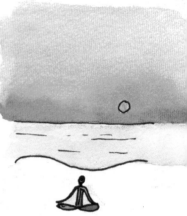

IT was PEaCEFuL aND HumBLINg
aND FREEINg, SomEHOW, To THINK
THaT mINE was ONLY ONE IN aN
aNCIENT LINE oF TRouBLED
mINDS THaT HaD ComE To THE
SEa FoR SOLaCE.

I was NOT THE FIRST
PERSON To STRUggLE —
NOR WOULD I BE THE LaST.

I LOOKED AT MY FEELINGS
IN A NEW WAY:
NOT THROUGH EYES OF
SELF-ABSORPTION AND
ISOLATION, BUT THROUGH
THE LONG LENS OF TIME AND
THE HUMBLING MIRROR OF
HUMAN COMMONALITY

AND SUDDENLY I
COULD SEE HOW
THEY WERE ALL
AS FLEETING AS
THE WAVES.

TAKE THIS BOOK OUTSIDE and
TURN ON your SENSES FOR a
FEW MINUTES. WRITE DOWN:

5 THINGS you SEE

① _____

② _____

③ _____

④ _____

⑤ _____

4 THINGS you HEAR

① _____

② _____

③ _____

④ _____

3 THINGS you FEEL

① _____

_____

② _____

③ _____

2 THINGS you SMELL

① _____

② _____

1 NEW THING you NOTICED

_____

TRY a WALKING MEDITATION

CHANGE YOUR SCENERY AND FIND SOMETHING LARGER THAN YOURSELF TO CONNECT TO AT THE SAME TIME WITH A WALKING MEDITATION.

YOU DO NOT NEED TO LIVE NEAR A HIKING TRAIL OR ON THE EDGE OF A BEAUTIFUL FOREST TO DO THIS.

TRY IT IN YOUR OWN NEIGHBORHOOD.

NO PARKING

AS YOU WALK, TURN YOUR ATTENTION TO THE FEEL OF YOUR FEET ON THE GROUND; YOUR SHOES ON THE PATH OR PAVEMENT. ARE YOU WALKING ON ASPHALT? A PEBBLY, LOOSE PATH? SOFT AND SPONGY GRASS?

NOTICE HOW AUTOMATIC IT IS TO WALK: ONE FOOT IN FRONT OF THE OTHER, OVER AND OVER.

YOU CAN FOCUS ON OTHER PHYSICAL SENSATIONS, TOO: THE GENTLE TOUCH OF WIND IN YOUR HAIR, THE WARMTH OF THE SUN THROUGH YOUR CLOTHES, THE SHARP BITE OF COLD AIR MOVING IN AND OUT OF YOUR NOSE.

REST YOUR ATTENTION ON THE SOUNDS ALL AROUND YOU: CHIRPING BIRDS, BUZZING INSECTS, THE NEIGHBOR'S LAWNMOWER. A BARKING DOG, FALLING RAIN, RUSH HOUR TRAFFIC.

LISTEN TO THE CONSTANT ORCHESTRA OF LITTLE NOISES THAT SURROUND YOU AS YOU WALK.

LET THEM WASH OVER YOU, KNOWING YOU CAN DO NOTHING TO MAKE THEM END OR BEGIN. THEY JUST ARE.

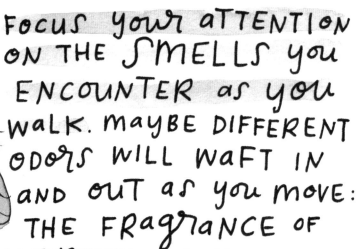

FOCUS YOUR ATTENTION ON THE SMELLS YOU ENCOUNTER AS YOU WALK. MAYBE DIFFERENT ODORS WILL WAFT IN AND OUT AS YOU MOVE: THE FRAGRANCE OF AN EVERGREEN HERE, A BLOOMING VINE THERE, CAR EXHAUST OVER THERE.

NOTICE THAT SOME SMELLS SEEM TO LINGER, WHILE OTHERS ARE FLEETING. DO SOME SMELLS FADE INTO THE BACKGROUND AFTER A WHILE? CAN YOU DETECT THEM AGAIN IF YOU TRY?

FOCUS ON YOUR OWN
FEELINGS.

HAVE THEY CHANGED SINCE
THE BEGINNING OF THIS
MEDITATION?

IN WHAT WAYS?

WERE YOU AWARE OF ANY
SHIFT AS IT WAS HAPPENING,
OR ONLY AFTERWARD?

COULD YOUR FEELINGS STILL
BE CHANGING, RIGHT NOW?

AS PART OF YOUR WALKING MEDITATION, FIND SOMETHING IN NATURE THAT YOU FIND INTERESTING OR BEAUTIFUL. DRAW OR TAPE IT HERE:

THINK aBOUT WHY you CHOSE
THIS OBJECT OVER EVERYTHING
ELSE you saw. WHaT maDE you
NOTICE IT? WHY DID you CONNECT
WITH IT? _____
_____
_____
_____
_____
_____
_____

WHaT DO you NOTICE WHEN you
REST youR mINDFUL aTTENTION
ON IT? _____
_____
_____
_____
_____
_____
_____

CHAPTER FIVE

give your FEELINGS a PLACE TO go

SOMETIMES I THINK OF
MY FEELINGS as actual
PHYSICAL ENTITIES,
EBBING and FLOWING and
SWIRLING around INSIDE me,
making
THEIR PRESENCE
KNOWN.

EACH ONE HAS ITS OWN
VOICE,
ITS OWN
PARTICULAR

MELANCHOLY

ENERGY SIGNATURE,
ITS OWN

ANXIETY

PURPOSE
FOR appearing
IN MY LIFE — EVEN IF
I DON'T UNDERSTAND
WHAT IT MIGHT BE.

EACH HAS ITS OWN
MESSAGE TO RELAY:
ITS OWN NEED TO BE
SEEN
AND HEARD.
AND SOMETIMES I CAN
HELP THEM EXPRESS
THEMSELVES A LITTLE
MORE CLEARLY BY GIVING
THEM A PLACE TO GO:

THIS PLACE.

THE BLANK PAGE — a SPACE
WHERE THE INTANGIBLE
CAN TAKE FORM.

CREATIVE WORK OPENS
a WINDOW
ONTO your
INNER
LANDSCAPE.

IT COAXES WHATEVER IS
PERCOLATING INSIDE you
OUT FROM ITS HIDING
PLACE. IT gaTHERS UP
aLL OF your CLaMorous
EMOTIONS aND gIVES THEM
a SPaCE To SPEaK THEIR
MESSaGES; a NEW CONTEXT
IN WHICH To maKE THEIR
PRESENCE KNOWN.

SOMETIMES GIVING YOUR FEELINGS a PLACE TO go HELPS you SEE THEM IN a NEW LIGHT, or UNDERSTAND THEM IN a WAY YOU DIDN'T BEFORE.

SOMETIMES IT'S JUST a RELEASE.

EITHER WAY...

CREATING SOMETHING IS a SACRED AND DEEPLY PERSONAL ACT. EVERY PIECE OF CREATIVE WORK YOU MAKE IS INHERENTLY AND IRREVOCABLY YOURS, STAMPED WITH YOUR ESSENCE, YOUR ENERGY— AN EMOTIONAL SIGNATURE, A PIECE OF YOURSELF ON A PAGE.

A BLANK PAGE
IS NOT THE ONLY PLACE
YOUR FEELINGS CAN GO,
OF COURSE.

CREATIVE EXPRESSION TAKES
MANY DIFFERENT FORMS:

FROM SINGING OR PLAYING
♪ AN INSTRUMENT

TO PLANTING A GARDEN

TO PERFORMING A DANCE

TO MAKING A MEME
OR A TIK TOK VIDEO

TO BAKING A CAKE.

CREATIVE WORK IS
ANYTHING YOU DO TO
BRING SOMETHING
INTO EXISTENCE THAT
DIDN'T EXIST BEFORE
AND WOULDN'T EXIST
BUT FOR YOU.

IT'S ANYTHING
YOU IMBUE WITH
YOUR UNIQUE
ENERGY, YOUR
EMOTIONAL SIGNATURE.

IT'S ANYTHING THAT GIVES AN OUTLET TO THE EXPRESSIVE INNER VOICE THAT ABIDES QUIETLY WITHIN YOU, WAITING FOR PERMISSION TO SPEAK.

ARE THERE ANY CREATIVE HOBBIES
YOU HAVE ALWAYS WANTED
TO TRY? EVEN IF YOU THINK
THEY WOULD BE DIFFICULT
OR INACCESSIBLE, BRAIN-
STORM A FEW AND WRITE
THEM DOWN: _____

CERAMICS

_____

_____

_____

_____

PHOTO-
GRAPHY

GLASS
BLOWING

_____

_____

_____

_____

JEWELRY
MAKING

PAINTING

POETRY

OF THE HOBBIES YOU WROTE DOWN, WHICH SEEM MOST ENTICING TO YOU?

BAKING

KNITTING

_____

_____

_____

_____

_____

_____

WEB DESIGN

CHALLENGE YOURSELF TO SPEND ONE HOUR THIS WEEK ON A CREATIVE ENDEAVOR. WRITE ABOUT HOW IT FELT TO EXPLORE: _____

_____

_____

_____

_____

INDOOR GARDENING

SCRAPBOOKING

LET GO OF JUDGMENT

OFTEN, THE THING THAT STOPS PEOPLE FROM EXPLORING THEIR CREATIVITY IS a SENSE THAT CREATIVE WORK IS NOT "FOR" THEM: THAT THE REALM OF CREATIVITY IS SOMEHOW LIMITED, aLL SPACE RESERVED FOR GENIUSES aND PROFESSIONALS aND THOSE OF GREAT TALENT; THAT CREATIVE WORK MUST BE "GOOD" TO BE WORTHWHILE.

THIS IS NONSENSE.
CREATIVE WORK IS FOR
EVERYONE.
IT'S AN INNATE THING you
WERE BORN KNOWING
HOW TO DO. IT
DOES NOT REQUIRE
TRAINING or KNOWLEDGE or
JUSTIFICATION. IT IS AN END
IN ITSELF — a METHOD OF
INTROSPECTING and PROCESSING,
a MEANS OF CHANNELING your
EMOTIONAL ENERGY INTO
SOMETHING TANGIBLE.

So LET go OF your EXPECTATIONS AND JUDGMENTS ABOUT WHAT you CREATE.

THIS WORK IS JUST FOR YOU, AND IT DOES NOT NEED TO BE PERFECT, or SKILLFUL, or a MASTERPIECE IN order TO BE a TOOL For HEALING.

HAVE you EVER TOLD yourSELF
THAT you'RE BaD aT DRAWING or
WRITING, or THAT you'RE NOT
VERy CREATIVE? WRITE DOWN
SoME OF THE JUDGMENTS you'VE
MaDE aBout your CREATIVE
aBILITIES: _____

_____
_____
_____
_____
_____
_____
_____
_____
_____
_____
_____
_____
_____

NOW SCRIBBLE OVER THEM
(aS aRTISTICaLLy aS POSSIBLE!♥)

HOW TO START making aRT

READY TO CREATE BUT NOT SURE HOW TO BEGIN? HERE are a FEW IDEAS:

THINK aBOUT THE KINDS OF aRT YOU ENJOYED making aS a KID. WHAT DID YOU LIKE WORKING WITH — CRAYONS or CLAY? WHAT DID YOU GET EXCITED TO SEE your aRT TEACHER SETTING OUT as you WALKED INTO CLASS?

DID YOU HAVE a FAVORITE SUBJECT? A SIGNATURE STYLE?

TAKE a FIELD TRIP TO THE ART SUPPLY STORE. WANDER THE AISLES AND SEE WHAT CAPTURES your INTEREST. ♥ SMELL ALL THE PAPER — AND THE PENCILS, TOO! TEST OUT ALL THE MARKERS. WHAT DRAWS YOU IN? WHAT LOOKS LIKE FUN? DON'T FEEL LIKE YOU HAVE TO SPEND a LOT OF MONEY, THOUGH. THIS TRIP IS FOR EXPLORING, AND IT'S NEVER a BAD IDEA TO...

START SIMPLE. YOU DON'T NEED EXPENSIVE SUPPLIES TO BE CREATIVE. YOU MIGHT EVEN HAVE THE MATERIALS YOU NEED AT HOME.

USE a PROMPT.

LISTS OF PROMPTS ABOUND ONLINE—
YOU CAN EVEN JOIN AN ART CHALLENGE
LIKE #INKTOBER. USE PROMPTS
OR CHALLENGES AS INSPIRATION,
OR POST YOUR WORK ONLINE
AND FIND A COMMUNITY OF OTHERS
WHO ARE DOING THE SAME!

INCORPORATE MINDFULNESS.

THE TEXTURE OF YOUR
PAPER, THE FEEL OF A
BRUSH IN YOUR HAND,
THE SLIMY SMOOTHNESS
OF CLAY UNDER YOUR
FINGERTIPS — THERE
ARE SO MANY PLACES
TO REST YOUR
ATTENTION AS
YOU CREATE.

THE WAY COLORS BLEND TOGETHER

FILL IN THE FOLLOWING PAGES
WITH YOUR OWN DOODLES —
EMBELLISH THE WATERCOLORS
THAT ARE ALREADY HERE, OR USE
THEM TO CREATE SOMETHING NEW.

A FEW art PROMPTS

① IF you WERE a PLANT or aN
aNimaL, WHaT WOULD you BE? DRaw
yoursELF IN your NaTuRaL HaBITaT.

② THINK OF a QUOTE or SONG
LyRIC THaT SPEaKS To you. DOODLE
THE QUOTE ITSELF, or SOME OF THE
ImaGES IT BRINGS TO mIND.

③ CREaTE a SELF—PoRTRaIT.
STICK FIGURES COUNT! LET
IT CONVEY SOMETHING
aBouT WHo you aRE.

④ DO a LITTLE DOODLING ON THE
SamE PIECE OF PaPER EVERY
Day — JUST a mINUTE OR TWO
aT a TIME — UNTIL IT'S FULL.

⑤ DRaw SOMETHING
you Saw IN a DREam.

EXPRESS yourself IN WRITING

A JOURNAL IS ANOTHER SAFE AND ILLUMINATING PLACE FOR YOUR FEELINGS TO GO. JOURNALING SERVES MANY PURPOSES:

- [ ] A PLACE TO VENT ANGER OR NEGATIVE THOUGHTS
- [ ] A CAPTURED HISTORY OF THE EXPERIENCES THAT SHAPE YOU
- [ ] A WAY TO ORGANIZE YOUR THOUGHTS
- [ ] A SAFE SPACE TO DO THE WORK OF UNLEARNING OLD HABITS & BELIEFS
- [ ] A PLACE TO PRACTICE REFRAMING YOUR EXPERIENCES
- [ ] A BLANK CANVAS FOR THINKING THROUGH A PROBLEM
- [ ] A TOOL FOR DEFINING PRIORITIES

SOME JOURNALING PRACTICES TO TRY

MORNING PAGES

THE BRILLIANT INVENTION OF JULIA CAMERON, AUTHOR OF THE ARTIST'S WAY, MORNING PAGES ARE 3 PAGES YOU WRITE BY HAND EACH MORNING BEFORE DOING ANYTHING ELSE. YOU CAN WRITE ABOUT WHATEVER YOU LIKE. IT DOESN'T MATTER — THIS IS NOT THE PLACE TO BE LYRICAL OR PROFOUND. (SOMETIMES MY MORNING PAGES SAY "I DON'T KNOW WHAT TO WRITE" FOR 10 LINES IN A ROW.) MORNING PAGES ARE SIMPLY A PRACTICE OF FILLING THE PAGES WITH WHATEVER COMES TO MIND — AND REVEALING TO YOURSELF WHAT'S BEEN ON YOUR MIND.

GRATITUDE JOURNAL

A GRATITUDE JOURNAL CAN HELP you FEEL BETTER BY INSPIRING you TO SEEK OUT AND ACKNOWLEDGE SOURCES OF JOY IN your LIFE. THE PRACTICE CAN BE SIMPLE — LIKE making a LIST OF 5 THINGS EACH DAY THAT MADE you SMILE, or 3 BEAUTIFUL THINGS you SAW. THE IDEA IS TO KEEP POSITIVITY AT THE FOREFRONT OF YOUR CONSCIOUSNESS, BOTH WHILE you WRITE AND AS you MOVE THROUGH your DAY, LOOKING FOR THINGS you CAN WRITE ABOUT.

DON'T WORRY ABOUT THE DAYS you CAN'T THINK OF ANYTHING TO WRITE. SOME DAYS ARE LIKE THAT. JUST COME BACK TO your JOURNAL WHEN you'RE READY.

EMOTIONAL CATHARSIS JOURNAL

COME TO YOUR JOURNAL THE NEXT TIME YOU ARE IN A HEIGHTENED EMOTIONAL STATE, AND WRITE. WRITE OUT EVERYTHING YOU'RE THINKING, THE WAY YOUR FEELINGS ARE SHOWING UP IN YOUR BODY, WHAT TRIGGERED YOUR FEELINGS, WHAT YOU'D LIKE TO DO ABOUT THEM.

OR, TRY DISSECTING A BIG FEELING AFTER THE FACT, WHEN YOU'RE FEELING CALMER. SOMETIMES YOU CAN SEE THINGS DIFFERENTLY WHEN YOU ARE REMOVED FROM THE OVERWHELMING IMMEDIACY OF YOUR EMOTIONS.

FILL THIS PAGE WITH WHAT—
EVER IS ON YOUR MIND RIGHT
NOW. IT DOESN'T MATTER WHAT
YOU WRITE — FEEL FREE TO
RAMBLE!

FOR THE NEXT 5 DAYS, FILL THE FOLLOWING PAGES WITH 3 THINGS THAT MADE YOU SMILE. IF NOTHING DOES, THAT'S OKAY! SKIP THAT DAY AND COME BACK WHEN YOU FEEL LIKE IT.

DATE: _____

① _____

② _____

③ _____

DATE: _____

① _____

② _____

③ _____

DaTE: _____

① _____

② _____

③ _____

DaTE: _____

① _____

② _____

③ _____

DaTE: _____

① _____

② _____

③ _____

CHAPTER SIX

SET yourSELF FREE

THERE'S a BUDDHIST TEACHING THAT aSKS you To IMAGINE THAT you aRE going aLong, ENJoying yourSELF and MINDING your own BUSINESS, WHEN SUDDENLY— OUT OF NOWHERE— you are STRUCK BY a FLYING arrow.

OUCH! THAT HURTS!

!

WTF

WHY ME

OF COURSE YOU'LL BE SHAKEN AND UPSET BY THE EXPERIENCE. THERE'S NO WAY NOT TO BE...

AND THAT'S WHEN THE SECOND *arrow* HITS.

NOW YOU'RE REALLY AGITATED

HEY! THAT HURTS EVEN MORE!

(AND IN CONSIDERABLY MORE PAIN).

AS BAD AS IT IS TO BE STRUCK BY AN *arrow*, BEING STRUCK BY TWO *arrows* IS UNDOUBTEDLY WORSE.

SO IF YOU COULD AVOID ONE OF THEM, WOULDN'T YOU WANT TO?

SOMETIMES IN LIFE,

WE CANNOT HELP BUT ENCOUNTER PAIN AND DIFFICULTY. AND WHEN WE DO, Two arrows FLY at US.

THE FIRST arrow IS THE MISFORTUNE ITSELF:

HOWEVER great or small, IT WILL BRING WITH IT SOME amount OF PAIN THAT CANNOT BE AVOIDED.

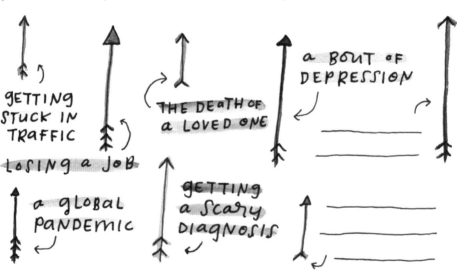

GETTING STUCK IN TRAFFIC

LOSING a JOB

a GLOBAL PANDEMIC

THE DEATH OF a LOVED ONE

GETTING a Scary DIAGNOSIS

a BOUT OF DEPRESSION

You MIGHT THEN REACT to your PAIN IN ways THAT CREATE UNNECESSARY ADDITIONAL SUFFERING.

THAT REACTION IS THE SECOND arrow,

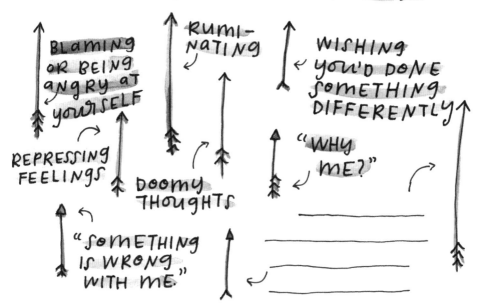

BLAMING OR BEING ANGRY AT YOURSELF

RUMI-NATING

WISHING YOU'D DONE SOMETHING DIFFERENTLY

REPRESSING FEELINGS

DOOMY THOUGHTS

"WHY ME?"

"SOMETHING IS WRONG WITH ME."

AND IT CAN BE JUST AS PAINFUL AS THE FIRST. MAYBE EVEN MORE SO.

BUT THERE IS good NEWS.

THE SECOND arrow

IS THE ONE you CAN avoid...

BECAUSE IT'S THE

arrow you
aim AT
yourself.

THE TRUTH IS, THE WORLD IS NOT a SAFE PLACE. IT IS a SCARY AND VULNERABLE THING TO GO ABOUT LIFE EVERY DAY AS a HUMAN.

YOU HAVE a MILLION SOFT AND TENDER SPOTS FOR ARROWS TO PENETRATE — AND, INEVITABLY, THEY WILL.

THERE IS NO WAY TO PROTECT YOURSELF FROM THE FIRST ARROW.

$\rightarrow\!\!\!\rightarrow$

BUT YOU CAN LEARN TO
REACT TO IT
WITH ACCEPTANCE
AND SELF-COMPASSION
RATHER THAN RESISTANCE
AND SELF-BLAME.

YOU CAN LEARN
TO AVOID
THE SECOND
arrow.

YOU CAN LEARN
TO SET
yourSELF
FREE.

ON
ACCEPTANCE

ACCEPTANCE WORKS KIND
OF LIKE armor against
THE SECOND arrow.

IT PROTECTS you FROM
THE SELF-IMPOSED
SUFFERING CAUSED BY
RESISTING REALITY—

BY WISHING THINGS
WERE DIFFERENT—

BY TELLING yourSELF
IT'S all your FAULT.

I KNOW I NEED TO WORK ON ACCEPTANCE WHEN I NOTICE MYSELF THINKING THINGS LIKE:

IF ONLY I COULD THINK OF THE RIGHT ARGUMENT, I COULD GET THEM TO CHANGE THEIR MIND.

WHY IS MY CHILD ACTING LIKE THIS? WHAT HAVE I DONE WRONG AS A PARENT?

WHY CAN'T THINGS JUST WORK?!

I DIDN'T DO ENOUGH TO HELP.

IF I'D MADE A DIFFERENT CHOICE, THINGS WOULD BE DIFFERENT NOW.

I HATE BEING TRAPPED IN THIS AGING BODY. I WISH I STILL HAD MY 21-YEAR-OLD KNEES.

THESE THOUGHTS are ALL WAYS OF TORMENTING MYSELF OVER THINGS — LIKE PAST DECISIONS AND OTHER PEOPLE'S BEHAVIOR AND EVEN THE AGING PROCESS THAT ARE NOT IN MY CONTROL.

SO WHY DO I TORMENT MYSELF?

AND IF I CAN'T
CONTROL THEM,

I CAN AT LEAST SAVE
MYSELF FROM SOME
PAIN BY WORKING TO
ACCEPT
THEM.

ACCEPTANCE IS
THE PRACTICE OF
ALLOWING REALITY
TO BE AS IT IS
INSTEAD OF
CREATING SUFFERING.
BY TRYING TO
RESIST IT.

OKAY... BUT WHAT DOES THAT
ACTUALLY MEAN? AM I SUPPOSED
TO MAGICALLY START LIKING
PAIN OR ENJOYING FAILURE?

NO!

ACCEPTANCE DOES
NOT MEAN:

LIKING SOMETHING.
AGREEING WITH IT.
APPROVING OF IT.
ENJOYING IT.

IT DOESN'T MEAN HAVING
PLEASANT FEELINGS
ABOUT UNPLEASANT
EXPERIENCES.

IT DOESN'T MEAN FORCING
a SMILE WHEN you
FEEL LIKE FROWNING,

or FAKING IT 'TIL you
MAKE IT.

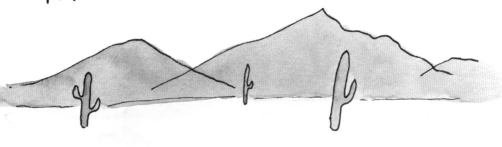

IT MEANS UNDERSTANDING THAT SOME THINGS — MANY THINGS! — ARE NOT IN YOUR POWER TO CHANGE OR CONTROL

AND SO, WHEN YOU BLAME YOUR-SELF FOR THEM ⟵————————⟪

⟫⟫⟫————⟶ OR THINK YOU ARE RESPONSIBLE FOR FIXING THEM

OR BURY THEM OR TRY TO WISH THEM AWAY ⟵————————⟪

YOU ONLY HURT YOURSELF.

ACCEPTANCE IS THE
PRACTICE OF EXTRICATING
YOURSELF FROM THIS FORM
OF SELF-HARM:

RELEASING YOURSELF
FROM AN OBLIGATION YOU
NEVER ACTUALLY HAD,

LAYING DOWN a BURDEN
THAT WAS NEVER REALLY
YOURS TO BEAR...
AND
SETTING
YOURSELF FREE.

WHAT'S SOMETHING you HAVE a HARD TIME ACCEPTING? _____

_____

_____

_____

HOW DO you WISH THINGS WERE INSTEAD? WRITE aBOUT IT IN aS muCH DETaIl aS POSSIBLE — REaLLy ENVISION aN IDEaL aLTERNaTE REaLITY: _____

_____

_____

_____

_____

_____

_____

_____

_____

_____

_____

IS THIS REALITY WITHIN your POWER
TO BRING ABOUT? WHY or WHY NOT?

_____

_____

_____

_____

_____

_____

_____

EXPERIMENT WITH LETTING go OF
your VISION OF an IDEAL REALITY.
maybe IMAGINE IT POPPING LIKE a
BUBBLE, or FLOATING away LIKE a
BalLOON. DO any FEELINGS come UP?

_____

_____

_____

_____

_____

a FEW WAYS TO PRACTICE ACCEPTANCE

DON'T "SHOULD" YOURSELF.

THE WORD "SHOULD" IS A ROADBLOCK ON THE PATH TO ACCEPTANCE.

I SHOULD BE ABLE TO DO THIS!

I SHOULDN'T HAVE SAID THAT.

IT SHOULDN'T BE THIS WAY.

IT POSES AS ASPIRATIONAL— EVEN HELPFUL— BUT IT IMPOSES GUILT & ASSIGNS BLAME. IF THINGS SHOULD BE A WAY THEY AREN'T, THEN SOMEONE MUST BE AT FAULT, AND IT'S EASY TO BELIEVE THAT SOMEONE IS YOU.

PRACTICE CONTROLLED DISCOMFORT

IT'S EASY TO BE ACCEPTING OF A PLEASANT OR COMFORTABLE SITUATION. YOU CAN PRACTICE ACCEPTING THE TOUGHER STUFF BY PUTTING YOURSELF IN SITUATIONS WHERE YOU FEEL UNCOMFORTABLE, BUT TOTALLY IN CONTROL:

GO SOLO TO A RESTAURANT OR MOVIE [ADMIT ONE]

 TRY OUT AN INTIMIDATING NEW HOBBY

PUSH PAST THE POINT WHERE YOU WOULD USUALLY QUIT IN YOUR WORKOUT

 TURN THE WATER TO COLD FOR THE LAST MINUTE OF YOUR SHOWER.

IF You NEED HELP SITTING WITH your DISCOMFORT, TRY:

♡ FOCUSING ON your BREaTH or DOING a BODY SCAN — NOTICE WHERE DISCOMFORT IS SHOWING UP.

♡ CONSCIOUSLY aND DELIBERaTELY RELAXING your BODY.

♥ OBSERVING any "SHOULDS," SELF-BlamE, or OTHER SECOND arrows.

♥ OFFERING yourSELF COMFORTING WORDS, LIKE "You arE SaFE. You arE STRONG. THIS IS HarD, aND you aRE IN CONTROL."

♥ALLOWING yourSELF To END THE EXPERIENCE THE INSTaNT you'VE HaD ENOugH.

DO THINGS POORLY

IF YOU FIND YOURSELF STRUGGLING TO DO THINGS UP TO SOME KIND OF STANDARD — ESPECIALLY WHEN YOU'RE GOING THROUGH a TOUGH TIME — TRY PRACTICING ACCEPTANCE BY ALLOWING YOUR-SELF TO DO THINGS POORLY. HALF-ASS TASKS. CUT CORNERS. ALLOW YOURSELF NOT TO BE ON YOUR A-GAME.

IF YOU KNOW YOU NEED TO BRUSH YOUR TEETH FOR TWO MINUTES BUT CAN'T MOTIVATE YOURSELF TO DO IT, BRUSH FOR 10 SECONDS INSTEAD — AND ACCEPT THAT IT'S ENOUGH. DOING SOMETHING POORLY IS BETTER THAN NOT DOING IT AT ALL.

ACCEPT THAT ACCEPTANCE IS a STRUGGLE.

IF YOU'RE HAVING a HARD TIME PRACTICING ACCEPTANCE...

DON'T WORRY ABOUT IT. IT'S HARD,
AND YOU'RE DOING GREAT. ♡

LEARNING TO LET GO OF RESISTANCE IS a massive paradigm SHIFT.

GIVE YOURSELF TIME, PATIENCE, AND SPACE FOR STRUGGLING as you LEARN THIS PRACTICE.

ARE THERE ANY TASKS YOU'VE
BEEN STRUGGLING WITH BECAUSE
THEY FEEL TOO OVERWHELMING?

_____
_____
_____
_____
_____
_____

WHAT MIGHT IT LOOK LIKE TO
DO THESE TASKS POORLY?

_____
_____
_____
_____
_____
_____

DID IT
POORLY

THIS IS a SPACE FOR CELEBRATING SMALL VICTORIES! WHAT ARE SOME OF YOUR RECENT ONES?

ON SELF-COMPASSION

ANOTHER WAY TO FREE
YOURSELF FROM THE STING
OF THE SECOND ARROW IS TO
PRACTICE SELF-COMPASSION:
TO OFFER YOURSELF COMFORT
AND KINDNESS WHEN YOU ARE
GOING THROUGH SOMETHING
DIFFICULT, INSTEAD OF HARSH
WORDS AND JUDGMENT.

SELF-COMPASSION LOOKS LIKE THIS:

THIS IS REALLY HARD. YOU'LL GET THROUGH IT, BUT IT'S OKAY TO STRUGGLE RIGHT NOW. I'M HERE FOR YOU. WHATEVER THE OUTCOME, WE'LL BE OKAY.

INSTEAD OF THIS:

WHY CAN'T YOU HANDLE THIS? YOU'RE SO WEAK! WHAT'S WRONG WITH YOU? GET IT TOGETHER!

IT'S TREATING MYSELF
WITH THE SAME KINDNESS,
ENCOURAGEMENT, AND
EMPATHY I WOULD OFFER
MY BEST FRIEND.

AND IT FEELS
REALLY WEIRD.

I ALWAYS FEEL FALSE AND
FALTERING AND AWKWARD
SAYING ♡ NICE THINGS
TO MYSELF INSTEAD OF

MEAN ONES. ♡

THE COMPASSION THAT NATURALLY ARISES FOR THE PEOPLE I LOVE

FEELS MOST UNNATURAL TO TRY TO CONJURE FOR MYSELF.

BUT I REMIND MYSELF THAT EVERYONE DESERVES COMPASSION.

(INCLUDING ME!)
(INCLUDING YOU!)

I REMIND MYSELF THAT I'M
LEARNING a WHOLE NEW
STYLE OF SELF-INTERACTION.

OF COURSE IT WILL FEEL
STRANGE AND UNFAMILIAR
AT FIRST.

I REMIND MYSELF THAT
I am growing
AND THAT GROWTH TAKES
TIME, AND PATIENCE,
AND (SELF-) COMPASSION.

IF YOU COULD SEND A MESSAGE OF ENCOURAGEMENT AND COMPASSION BACK THROUGH TIME TO YOUR CHILD SELF, WHAT WOULD YOU SAY? :

HOW ABOUT TO YOUR ADOLESCENT SELF?

YOUR FIVE-YEARS-ago SELF?

_____
_____
_____
_____
_____
_____
_____
_____
_____

NOW CaN you SEND a mESSagE OF COmPaSSION TO yourSELF JUST aS you aRE, RIGHT NOW?

_____
_____
_____
_____
_____
_____
_____

GIVE yourself a FEW compliments. You DESERVE THEm.

WHAT SELF-COMPASSION ISN'T:

A WAY TO BE HAPPY ALL THE TIME.

SELF-COMPASSION DOESN'T MEAN YOU WON'T STILL FEEL BAD. IT JUST MEANS YOU HOLD YOURSELF IN LOVE AND SUPPORT RATHER THAN JUDGMENT AND BLAME WHEN YOU DO.

A PEP TALK.

SELF—COMPASSION IS NOT PSYCHING YOURSELF UP TO MOVE PAST a BAD FEELING. IT'S NOT aBOUT GETTING YOURSELF TO "CHEER UP!" or "MOVE ON!"

IT'S aN aCT OF SITTING WITH YOURSELF THROUGH YOUR DISTRESS, ALLOWING aLL YOUR BaD FEELINGS TO EXIST, OFFERING YOURSELF COMFORT THROUGH YOUR PAIN.

SOMETHING you EaRN.

SELF-COMPASSION IS NOT RESERVED FOR THOSE WHO NEVER MaKE MISTAKES. You aRE aLWAYS WORTHY OF SELF-COMPASSION.

EASY.

MOST OF US AREN'T IN THE HABIT OF OFFERING OURSELVES COMPASSION, AND IT TAKES LOTS OF WORK TO BREAK OLD AND AUTOMATIC PATTERNS OF

SELF-TALK.

I CATCH MYSELF IN MY OLD, UNHELPFUL HABITS ALL THE TIME.

OMG! I CAN'T EVEN DO SELF—COMPASSION RIGHT!

AND WHEN I DO, I TRY TO REMEMBER NOT TO BE ANGRY WITH MYSELF. I REMEMBER THAT THIS WORK IS HARD — AND I DESERVE COMPASSION AS I DO IT.

IF YOU'RE GOING THROUGH A TOUGH TIME AND NEED SOME COMPASSION, TRY FILLING IN THE BLANKS AND READING THIS LETTER ALOUD TO YOURSELF.

♥ DEAR _____,

I'm SO SORRY YOU ARE GOING THROUGH _____
_____.

YOU MUST BE FEELING SO _____, _____
AND _____,
AND THOSE ARE SUCH DIFFICULT WAYS TO FEEL. I'M ON YOUR SIDE THROUGH THIS. YOU'RE NOT ALONE, EVEN IF YOU FEEL LIKE IT.
LOVE,
_____

♥ ♥

TRY a SELF-COMPASSION MEDITATION

SIT IN a CALM, QUIET PLACE. GET COMFORTABLE. RELAX YOUR BODY, AND FEEL YOUR BREATH MOVE IN AND OUT. WHEN YOUR MIND WANDERS, REDIRECT IT TO THE BREATH.

WHEN YOU ARE READY, YOU MIGHT BEGIN REPEATING A MANTRA, LIKE:

MAY I BE SAFE. MAY I BE FREE FROM SUFFERING. MAY I BE AT EASE.

FEEL THE WEIGHT OF THE WORDS SETTLE INTO you as you BREATHE.

FEEL THEIR KIND and LOVING INTENTIONS RUSHING INTO your LUNGS WITH EVERY BREATH. PICTURE your BODY BEGINNING TO GLOW as your compassion FLOWS THROUGH IT.

EXTEND your COMPASSION TO SOMEONE you LOVE.

PICTURE THEM IN your MIND'S EYE AND WISH THEM ALL good THINGS.

May your DEAR ONE BE SAFE. May THEY BE FREE FROM SUFFERING.

May THEY BE AT EASE.

TAKE a FEW BREaTHS
aND SEE IF you CaN gROW
your compassion
EVEN LargER:

So LaRgE IT REaCHES
FRIENDS, aCQUAINTANCES,
STRANGERS — So gREaT
aND EXPaNSIVE IT COVERS
THE WHOLE WoRLD.

May ALL BEINgS BE SaFE. May
THEY BE FREE FROm SUFFERINg.
May THEY BE aT EaSE.

FEEL your
COMPASSION
RADIaTE
ouTWarD.

FINALLY, TRY EXTENDING
your compassion to
SOMEONE you DISLIKE:
an EX, an ESTRANGED FRIEND
or RELATIVE, THE PERSON WHO
CUT YOU OFF IN TRAFFIC EARLIER.

TRY TO SEE THEIR
HUMANITY ——
THAT THEY EXPERIENCE
THE Same SUFFERING you DO.

WISH THEM WELL (IF you CAN).

May your ENEMY BE SaFE.
MAY THEY BE FREE FROm
SUFFERING. May THEY BE aT EaSE.

KNOW THAT NOT ALL OF THE FEELINGS THAT ARISE IN THIS MEDITATION may BE PLEASANT AND WARM.

THIS IS a CHALLENGING EXERCISE, AND IT CAN EVOKE DIFFICULT, RAW, AND INTENSE EMOTIONS.

SIT WITH THEM AS THEY ARISE. REMEMBER THEY ARE ALL WELCOME AND OKAY. AND WHEN YOU FEEL READY, END YOUR MEDITATION ON A NOTE OF SELF-COMPASSION:

May YOU BE AT EASE. ♡

WHAT COLOR IS YOUR COMPASSION?
AS YOU COLOR THIS PAGE, IMAGINE
your COMPASSION RADIATING
out.

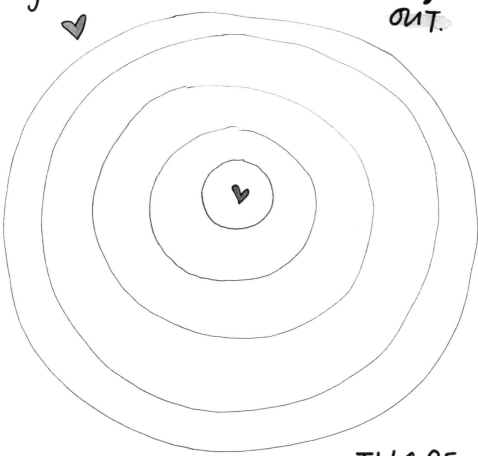

FILL IN THE NAMES OF THOSE
TO WHOM you SEND COMPASSION.

SOME SELF-COMPASSION PRACTICES TO TRY

TALK TO YOURSELF as you WOULD a DEAR FRIEND OR a SMALL CHILD

TAKE YOUR-SELF OUT ON a DATE

LISTEN TO MUSIC you LOVE

you HAVE NOTHING TO BE SORRY FOR.

WRITE your-SELF a LETTER OF FORGIVENESS

GIVE YOUR BODY a LITTLE massage WHERE IT FEELS TENSE

GIVE YOUR-SELF SPACE TO BREATHE.

(TRY a FOAM ROLLER)

YOU DO NOT HAVE TO ACT RIGHT NOW.

PART THREE

GETTING HELP WITH your FEELINGS

SOMETIMES THINGS
ARE SO DIFFICULT

NIGHTS SO ENDLESS

JOY AND HOPE SUCH
FORGOTTEN STRANGERS

THAT YOU CAN NO LONGER
GO IT ALONE.

IT'S OKAY TO NEED EXTRA HELP. IN FACT, THAT HELP CAN SOMETIMES MAKE THE DIFFERENCE BETWEEN a LIFE OF SUFFERING AND a LIFE OF JOY (MAYBE EVEN BETWEEN LIFE AND DEATH.)

AND YET

EVERY TIME I HAVE SOUGHT THAT EXTRA HELP IN THERAPY,

IT HAS BEEN WITH a SENSE OF SHAME, a FEELING OF BROKENNESS.

BUT THIS IS NOT a SPACE OF BROKENNESS.

IT IS a SPACE OF HEALING.

IT IS a PLACE To LEARN
Tools FOR SELF-STUDY
aND SELF-EXPRESSION.

A PLACE To RECEIVE THE gIFTS
OF EXPANSIVENESS aND
FORGIVENESS, aCCEPTaNCE
aND COMPaSSION.

A PLACE THAT HELPS you
SEE HoW much you
DESERVE THEM.

A PLACE THAT HELPS you
FEEL BETTER.

CHAPTER SEVEN

GETTING STARTED WITH THERAPY

I HAVE SPENT ALMOST 20 YEARS IN AND OUT OF THERAPY.

FOR MOST OF THEM, I THOUGHT OF THERAPY AS MY

DEEP, DARK SECRET.

I HOPE NOBODY SEES ME HERE

THERAPIST

I HID IT FROM MY FRIENDS.

FRIDAY? I CAN'T, I'M SEEING my... DOCTOR...

OK.

OH YES EVERYTHING IS FINE, I am DEFINITELY NOT FALLING aPART AND TO PROVE IT I BOUGHT THIS NEW PLANT.

I PRETENDED EVERYTHING WAS okay WHEN IT VERY MUCH WASN'T.

I CAN HIDE MY FACE BEHIND THAT magazine IF I NEED TO.

I WORRIED ABOUT RUNNING INTO SOMEONE I KNEW IN THE WAITING ROOM.

I WAS ASHAMED OF NEEDING HELP, BECAUSE I WAS BUYING INTO THE

MENTAL HEALTH STIGMA →

YOU'RE NUTS!

YOU'VE PROBABLY HEARD THE MENTAL HEALTH STIGMA BEFORE, BECAUSE IT'S EVERYWHERE. IT SAYS STUFF LIKE:

THERAPY IS FOR CRAZY PEOPLE!

YOU DON'T HAVE IT THAT BAD!

YOU HAVE TO PAY SOMEONE TO LISTEN TO YOU COMPLAIN?

THERAPY IS SO EMBARRASSING.

TRANSLATION:

MENTAL HEALTH ISSUES AREN'T REAL, OR AREN'T SERIOUS.

THERAPY IS FOR WEAK PEOPLE.

You SHOULD FEEL ASHAMED.

THE MENTAL HEALTH STIGMA IS SO TREACHEROUS BECAUSE IT **BLAMES** you FOR your OWN SUFFERING EVEN AS you DO EVERYTHING IN your POWER TO TRY TO FEEL BETTER.

THAT LOOKS LIKE a "you" PROBLEM.

AND IT makes THERAPY—
THE VERY THING THAT
COULD HELP!—FEEL
SHamEFuL, aND
DauNTINg, aND LIKE a
DEEP, DaRK SECRET.

BUT HERE'S THE THING.

EVERYONE SuFFERS.
EVERYONE STRuggLES.

EVEN IF you'RE DOINg
EVERYTHINg "RIGHT"...

I MEDITaTE, I JouRNaL, I EXERCISE,
I STILL FEEL REaLLy BaD.

SOMETIMES YOU STILL
NEED a LITTLE
EXTRa HELP,

AND THERaPY IS a GREaT
PLACE TO FIND IT.

NOT a DEEP, DaRk
SECRET,
BUT a COURaGEOUS
aCT OF SELF-CaRE.

HAVE you HEARD THE VOICE OF THE MENTAL HEALTH STIGMA? FILL IN WHAT IT'S SAID TO you:

WHAT WOULD you LIKE TO Say Back?

IS IT TIME To

You are in crisis, actively dealing with trauma, grief, or a difficult life event

You want to go

You feel hopeless and misunderstood

Your other self-care practices aren't really helping

You just feel blah

You're turning to coping mechanisms you know are unhealthy for you

TRY THERAPY?

You CAN'T STOP THINKING DISTURBING OR INTRUSIVE THOUGHTS

You NEED SOME EXTRA SUPPORT

SOMEONE you TRUST HAS EXPRESSED CONCERN OR SUGGESTED THERAPY

THERAPY CAN HELP!

You'RE CURIOUS ABOUT IT

You FEEL LIKE maybE IT COULD HELP

You COULD USE SOME PERSPECTIVE

HAVE YOU EVER WANTED TO TRY
THERAPY, BUT FOUND SOMETHING
HOLDING YOU BACK? WRITE ABOUT IT:

_____
_____
_____
_____
_____
_____
_____
_____
_____
_____
_____
_____
_____
_____
_____
_____
_____

HOW COULD YOU OVERCOME THE OBSTACLE(S) YOU JUST EXPRESSED? WRITE YOUR IDEAS DOWN:

_____
_____
_____
_____
_____
_____
_____
_____
_____
_____
_____
_____
_____
_____
_____
_____
_____

a map OF THE THERapy Room

A HINT at your THERapist's INTERESTS & PERSONALITY

SOMETHING THAT INSPIRES growth

LOTS OF BOOKS

A CLOCK you CAN SEE (DISCREETLY)

A CLOCK your THERapist CAN SEE (DISCREETLY)

YOUR SEAT (NOT always a COUCH)

YOUR THERapist's SEAT

TISSUES (IMPORTANT)

A PLACE FOR USED TISSUES

ON FINDING THE RIGHT THERAPIST

WHAT TRANSPIRES IN THE THERAPY ROOM IS SACRED AND INTIMATE AND DEEPLY VULNERABLE. YOU ARE THERE TO TALK ABOUT PAIN, TRAUMA, DESPAIR — TO OPEN YOUR HEART AND LAY OUT ITS CONTENTS FOR ANOTHER PERSON TO EXAMINE — TO RECEIVE THEIR HELP IN MAKING SOMETHING NEW OUT OF IT ALL.

YOU CAN'T DO THAT WITH JUST ANYONE!

THE RIGHT THERAPIST IS LIKE a PERSONAL GUIDE ON YOUR INNER JOURNEY:

A BOLD ONE, UNAFRAID TO SHINE a LIGHT INTO THE DARK RECESSES YOU WOULD RATHER AVOID.

A REASSURING ONE, HELPING YOU COPE WITH EVERYTHING YOU FIND THERE.

I KNOW YOU CAN'T ALWAYS SEE HOW STRONG YOU ARE. BUT I SEE IT.

AN EMPOWERING ONE, GIVING YOU THE TOOLS TO HELP YOU GROW — IN SESSION AND OUT OF IT.

KEYS TO A GREAT THERAPY RELATIONSHIP

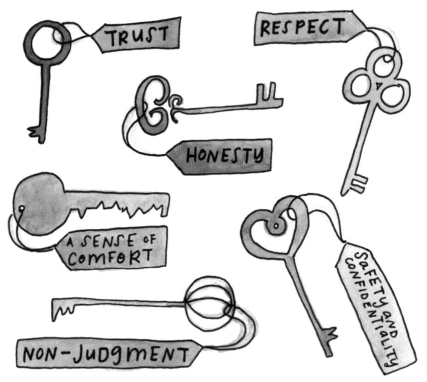

TRUST

RESPECT

HONESTY

A SENSE OF COMFORT

Safety and Confidentiality

NON-JUDGMENT

YOUR THERAPIST DOESN'T HAVE TO BE YOUR FAVORITE PERSON ON EARTH, BUT IF YOUR RELATIONSHIP LACKS ANY OF THESE KEY QUALITIES, YOU MIGHT HAVE A HARD TIME MAKING PROGRESS.

A THERAPIST WISH LIST

WHAT ARE YOU LOOKING FOR IN A THERAPIST? CHECK ALL THAT APPLY:

☐ SOMEONE WITH EXPERTISE IN YOUR ISSUES

☐ SOMEONE WHO SHARES YOUR BELIEFS OR IDENTITY

☐ SOMEONE WHO OFFERS A PARTICULAR TYPE OF THERAPY

☐ SOMEONE NEARBY

☐ SOMEONE THREE TOWNS OVER WHERE NOBODY KNOWS YOU

☐ SOMEONE WHO ASSIGNS LOTS OF HOMEWORK

☐ SOMEONE AFFORDABLE

☐ SOMEONE WHO LISTENS WELL

☐ _____

☐ _____

☐ _____

☐ _____

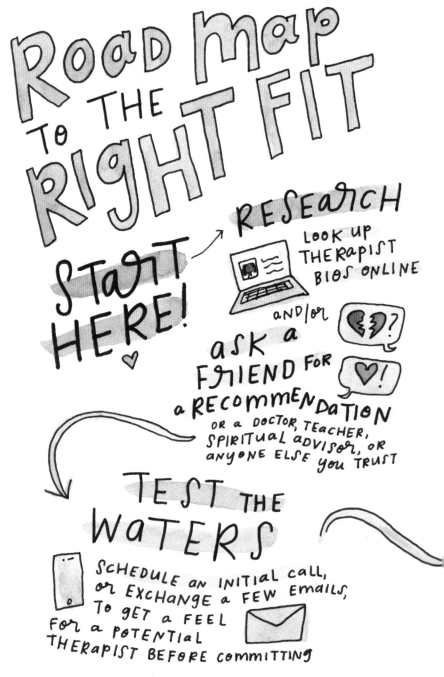

Road map to the RIGHT FIT

START HERE! ♥

RESEARCH
Look up THERAPIST BIOS ONLINE

aND/or 💔?

ask a FRIEND FOR a RECOMMENDATION ♥!
OR a DOCTOR, TEACHER, SPIRITUAL ADVISOR, OR ANYONE ELSE YOU TRUST

TEST THE WATERS
SCHEDULE an INITIAL call, or EXCHANGE a FEW EMAILS, TO GET a FEEL FOR a POTENTIAL THERAPIST BEFORE COMMITTING

BE WILLING TO make a CHANGE

IT'S ALWAYS OKAY TO TRY SOMEONE ELSE. YOUR THERAPIST WANTS YOU TO FIND THE RIGHT FIT, TOO!

TREAT YOURSELF WITH CARE

FINDING THE RIGHT FIT ISN'T EASY, SO DON'T LOSE HOPE. YOU'RE WORTH IT.

CHECK IN WITH YOURSELF

NOTICE HOW THERAPY MAKES YOU FEEL— BEFORE, DURING, AND AFTER SESSIONS.

TRY a FEW SESSIONS

TAKE A FEW WEEKS TO GET TO KNOW YOUR NEW THERAPIST BEFORE JUDGING.

IF you are CONSIDERING THERapy,
FILL IN THE BLANKS:

I'LL go To THERAPY WHEN _____
_____
_____
_____

THE THING aBouT THERAPY THAT
SCARES ME MOST IS _____
_____
_____
_____
_____

THE THING aBouT THERAPY THAT
EXCITES ME MOST IS _____
_____
_____
_____
_____
_____

IN THERAPY, I'D LIKE TO LEARN

_____
_____
_____
_____
_____
_____

I HOPE THERAPY HELPS ME _____

_____
_____
_____
_____
_____
_____
_____

IF YOU ARE ALREADY IN THERAPY (OR AFTER YOU START), FILL IN THE BLANKS:

I STARTED THERAPY BECAUSE _____
_____
_____
_____
_____

THERAPY FEELS BAD WHEN _____
_____
_____
_____
_____

THERAPY FEELS GOOD WHEN _____
_____
_____
_____
_____
_____
_____
_____
_____

IN THERAPY, I'VE LEARNED _____

_____

_____

_____

_____

_____

_____

_____

_____

_____

THERAPY IS HELPING ME _____

_____

_____

_____

_____

_____

_____

_____

_____

_____

_____

CHAPTER EIGHT

DOING THE WORK

THERAPY IS WORK.

IT'S HARD WORK.

IT'S CONFRONTING WORK.

IT'S INTENSE WORK.

THERE'S NO RIGHT WAY TO FEEL WHILE YOU'RE DOING THE DIFFICULT WORK OF THERAPY— AND IT DEFINITELY DOESN'T ALWAYS FEEL GOOD.

SOMETIMES IT MAKES ME FEEL LIKE I'M A STILL AND QUIET POND THAT GETS STIRRED UP SUDDENLY, LIKE ALL THE MUCK THAT HAS SETTLED TO THE BOTTOM, IGNORED FOR YEARS, IS YANKED TO THE SURFACE, LEAVING ME FEELING MUDDLED AND MURKY AND GROSS.

SOMETIMES IT MAKES ME
FEEL NAKED AND EXPOSED,
TENDER AND RAW:
I'LL SPEND THE REST
OF THE DAY WITH MY
EMOTIONS ROILING JUST
BELOW THE SURFACE, READY TO
SPILL OVER AT a MOMENT'S
NOTICE.

SOMETIMES IT MAKES
        ME FEEL HOLLOW:
    NUMB AND SPENT
        AND QUIETLY
        EMPTY.

I USED TO THINK SOMETHING WAS WRONG WHEN I FELT WORSE AFTER a SESSION,

SHOULDN'T THERAPY BE making ME FEEL BETTER?

LIKE mayBE IT was a SIGN THAT THERaPY WasN'T WoRKING. BuT I'VE LEaRNED IT usually MEaNS THE OPPOSITE: WHEN I FEEL murKY aND TENDER aND RaW, IT'S BECaUSE I am DOING THE WoRK OF DEALING WITH DIFFICULT THINGS INSTEaD OF EVaDING THEM — PROCESSING DIFFICULT FEELINGS INSTEaD OF IGNoRING THEM. ♡

THE WORK OF THERAPY IS
NOT EASY TO DO.

AND THE REWARDS OF THE
WORK ARE OFTEN SUBTLE,
AND AMBIGUOUS, AND SLOW
IN COMING.

BUT MAYBE, OVER TIME,
YOU'LL NOTICE YOU FEEL A
LITTLE BETTER: A BIT
LIGHTER, A LITTLE LESS RAW.

YOU MIGHT NOTICE
THAT THE WORK—
HEAVY AND DIFFICULT
AND WORTH DOING—
IS WORKING.

ARE THERE ANY THOUGHTS, FEELINGS, OR EXPERIENCES YOU'D LIKE TO ADDRESS IN THERAPY? _____

_____

_____

_____

_____

_____

_____

_____

_____

_____

_____

_____

WHAT DO YOU THINK WORKING THROUGH THEM MIGHT FEEL LIKE?

_____

_____

_____

_____

ARE THERE ANY THOUGHTS, FEELINGS, or EXPERIENCES YOU'RE AFRAID TO ADDRESS IN THERAPY? (IF YOU CAN'T WRITE THEM DOWN, JUST THINK ABOUT THEM.)

_____
_____
_____
_____
_____
_____
_____
_____
_____
_____

WHAT DO YOU THINK IT MIGHT FEEL LIKE TO WORK THROUGH THEM?

_____
_____
_____
_____
_____
_____
_____
_____

THE WORK OF CHANGE

WITHOUT a DOUBT, THERAPY CREATES CHANGE— BUT MAYBE NOT ALWAYS IN THE WAYS YOU EXPECT.

ONE OF THE REASONS I STARTED THERAPY WAS TO GET HELP WITH MY ANGER.

I GET WORKED UP — I LOSE MY TEMPER— I YELL AT PEOPLE I LOVE — AND I HATE ALL OF IT.

I HOPED THERAPY
WOULD HELP ME CHANGE:

BECOME SOMEONE WHO
IS NOT ANGRY

SOMEONE WHO HANDLES
EVERYTHING WITH
IMPLACABLE CALM

SOMEONE WHO
NEVER YELLS

SO WHEN I FOUND MYSELF SITTING ACROSS FROM MY THERAPIST ONE DAY, AFTER OVER A YEAR OF SESSIONS, TELLING HER ABOUT HOW I'D YELLED AT MY KIDS YET AGAIN,

I WONDERED: IS THIS EVEN WORKING?

WE'D SPENT COUNTLESS HOURS TALKING THROUGH MY ANGER AND STILL I'D YELLED. NOTHING HAD CHANGED.

MAYBE I CAN'T CHANGE.

WELL... SHE said,

You KIND OF CAN'T.

WHAT?

BUT THAT DOESN'T MATTER.

Again, WHAT?

IT DOESN'T MATTER IF YOU CAN'T CHANGE YOUR ANGER. YOU'RE A HUMAN — YOUR ANGER IS A HUMAN FEELING. YOU CAN'T EXPECT YOURSELF TO NEVER LOSE YOUR TEMPER. IT WILL ALWAYS HAPPEN SOMETIMES.

WHAT ACTUALLY MATTERS IS WHAT YOU CHOOSE TO DO NEXT.

So... WHAT DID YOU DO NEXT?

I TOLD HER ABOUT HOW I'D GONE TO MY KIDS—APOLOGIZED—EXPLAINED I WAS WRONG TO YELL—HUGGED THEM.

GREAT! MY THERAPIST BEAMED.

YOU DID THE BEST THING YOU COULD HAVE DONE. NICE JOB.

WOULDN'T THE BEST THING HAVE BEEN NOT TO YELL IN THE FIRST PLACE?

SURE... THAT'S ALWAYS THE GOAL. BUT DO YOU REALLY EXPECT YOURSELF TO NEVER MAKE A MISTAKE? TO MEET YOUR GOAL EVERY TIME?

OR CAN YOU ACCEPT THAT SOMETIMES YOU YELL? CAN YOU LET YOURSELF BE HUMAN IN THAT WAY?

LIKE IT OR NOT, YOUR ANGER IS PART OF WHO YOU ARE, AND WE'RE NOT WORKING TO CHANGE IT.

WE'RE WORKING TO COEXIST WITH IT. TO HANDLE IT IN HEALTHY WAYS.

I LEFT THERAPY THAT DAY aND LET THIS NEW PERSPECTIVE ROLL aROUND IN MY HEAD—THIS IDEa THaT THERaPY WaS NOT aBOUT CHANGING MYSELF

BUT RATHER aBOUT MEETING MYSELF WHERE I aM

aND WORKING WITH WHAT I HAVE.

TO ACCEPT THAT THE PARTS OF MYSELF I DON'T LIKE WILL ALWAYS EXIST ALONGSIDE THE PARTS I DO —

TO GIVE MYSELF SOME BREATHING ROOM BY MAKING SPACE FOR ALL OF THEM.

FOR ME, THERAPY HAS NOT
CREATED CHANGE
SO MUCH AS IT HAS CREATED
SPACE FOR ACCEPTANCE.

AND MAYBE THAT IS THE
VERY SPACE FROM WHICH
REAL CHANGE SPRINGS,
LIKE WATER TRICKLING
THROUGH ROCK:
SLOW AND SUBTLE
AND UTTERLY TRANSFORMATIVE.

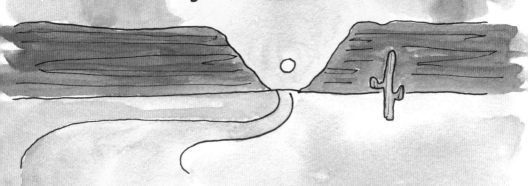

WHAT'S SOMETHING ABOUT
yourSELF you'D LIKE TO
CHANGE? _____

_____
_____
_____
_____
_____
_____
_____

DO you THINK THIS IS SOMETHING
you CAN ACTUALLY CHANGE? or
SOMETHING LIKELY TO KEEP
COMING UP? _____

_____
_____
_____
_____
_____

IF THIS IS SOMETHING YOU THINK
MIGHT KEEP ARISING, DO YOU
HAVE ANY IDEAS FOR HOW TO
HANDLE IT THE NEXT TIME IT DOES?

_____

_____

_____

_____

_____

_____

_____

_____

DO YOU THINK YOU CAN FIND
PEACE WITH IT — OR IMAGINE
FINDING PEACE WITH IT SOMEDAY?

_____

_____

_____

_____

_____

_____

THERAPY DO'S & DON'TS

DO KNOW your THERAPIST WILL KEEP THE THINGS you TELL THEM CONFIDENTIAL.

DO FEEL FREE TO USE as MANY TISSUES as you NEED. (YOUR THERAPIST HAS more!)

DON'T FEEL OBLIGATED TO STICK WITH a THERAPIST you DISLIKE, and **DON'T** SETTLE FOR SOMEONE WHO FEELS WRONG.

DON'T FEEL LIKE you HAVE TO TELL THEM **EVERYTHING** RIGHT away. SOME THINGS TAKE TIME & COURAGE TO REVEAL.

DO TELL THEM THE UNCOMFORTABLE, awkward STUFF you KNOW you NEED TO TALK about (EVEN THOUGH IT FEELS BAD).

DO REMEMBER THERE'S NO SUCH THING as a WASTED SESSION (EVEN IF you FEEL LIKE you DIDN'T TALK about anyTHING ImportANT).

DO KNOW SOME OF THE HARDEST WORK OF THERAPY IS IN SHOWING UP and OPENING UP.

SHOWED UP♥

DO EXPECT RANDOM FLOODS OF TEARS AND OTHER SUDDEN, STRONG EMOTIONS... AND

SERIOUSLY... I HAVE EXTRA TISSUES. LOTS.

DON'T FEEL WEIRD ABOUT THEM. Your THERAPIST HAS SEEN IT BEFORE.

DO THE HOMEWORK your THERAPIST ASSIGNS AS BEST you CAN, BUT **DON'T** SWEAT

THOUGHT RECORD

GRATITUDE JOURNAL

IT IF THERE ARE DAYS OR WEEKS you DON'T MAKE IT HAPPEN. JUST KEEP SHOWING UP. ♡

TODAY IN THERAPY I...

- ☐ LAUGHED ☐ CRIED ☐ YELLED
- ☐ OPENED UP ☐ CLOSED UP
- ☐ FELT BETTER AND/OR ☐ WORSE
- ☐ FELT SEEN AND/OR ☐ MISUNDERSTOOD
- ☐ FELT BRAVE AND/OR ☐ TIMID
- ☐ FELT _____ ☐ FELT _____
- ☐ FELT WORSE, BUT I KNOW LATER I'LL FEEL BETTER

☐ LEARNED SOMETHING: _____

_____

_____

_____

☐ UNDERSTOOD SOMETHING: _____

_____

_____

_____

ON MEDICATION ♥

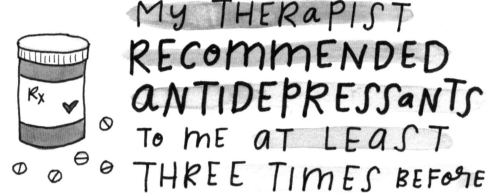

MY THERAPIST RECOMMENDED ANTIDEPRESSANTS TO ME AT LEAST THREE TIMES BEFORE I ACTUALLY LISTENED TO HER AND MADE AN APPOINTMENT WITH MY DOCTOR TO GET THEM.

EVERY TIME SHE MADE THE SUGGESTION, I WOULD THINK:

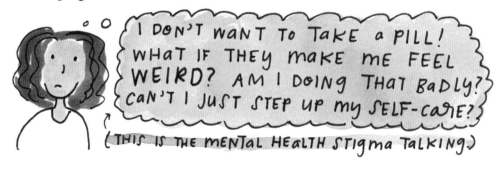

I DON'T WANT TO TAKE A PILL! WHAT IF THEY MAKE ME FEEL WEIRD? AM I DOING THAT BADLY? CAN'T I JUST STEP UP MY SELF-CARE?

(THIS IS THE MENTAL HEALTH STIGMA TALKING.)

I WOULD PUT MY THERAPIST'S ADVICE OUT OF MY MIND AND KEEP TRYING TO PULL MYSELF UP BY MY BOOTSTRAPS. I GOT THIS. (NOT RECOMMENDED.)

BY THE THIRD TIME SHE MENTIONED THEM, THOUGH, I... GOT THIS? IT WAS PRETTY CLEAR TO ME THAT MY "BOOTSTRAPS" METHOD WASN'T WORKING.

AND I FINALLY LISTENED.

HI, I'M CALLING FOR AN APPOINTMENT TO DISCUSS GOING ON ANTIDEPRESSANTS.

(THIS IS BRAVERY TALKING!)

I FELT KIND OF WEIRD
TAKING THE FIRST FEW PILLS,
NOT KNOWING HOW
THEY WOULD WORK,
HOW THEY MIGHT
ALTER HOW I FEEL...

... BUT AFTER A FEW DAYS, I
DIDN'T FEEL ALL THAT DIFFERENT.

EXCEPT I WAS FINALLY
ABLE TO SLEEP AFTER
WEEKS OF INSOMNIA.

AFTER A COUPLE OF WEEKS, I
DIDN'T FEEL ALL THAT DIFFERENT.

EXCEPT I NOTICED I WAS A
LITTLE LESS REACTIVE, A LITTLE
MORE EVEN-KEELED.

AFTER a COUPLE moRE WEEKS,
I DIDN'T FEEL aLL THaT DIFFERENT.

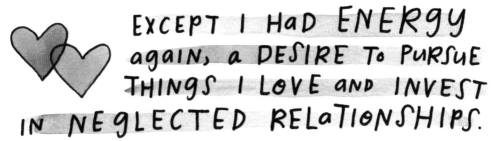

EXCEPT I HaD ENERGY
again, a DESIRE To PURSUE
THINGS I LOVE aND INVEST
IN NEGLECTED RELaTIONSHIPS.

I DIDN'T FEEL aLL THaT DIFFERENT...
EXCEPT I WaS INTERESTED
IN LIVING mY LIFE aGaIN.

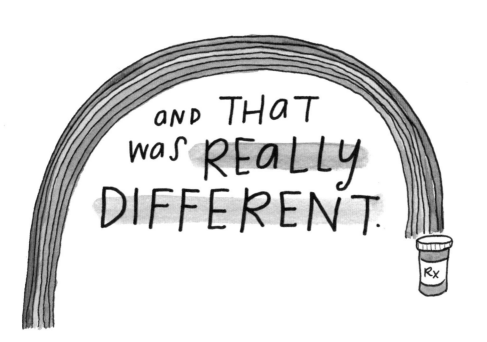

aND THAT
WaS REALLY
DIFFERENT.

MY MEDICATION DIDN'T
MAKE ME FEEL ALL THAT
DIFFERENT
BECAUSE IT WAS HELPING
ME FEEL MORE LIKE
MYSELF:
MY OLD SELF, THE
PERSON I'VE ALWAYS BEEN

THE PERSON DEPRESSION
HAD STOLEN.

I THINK MY THERAPIST
COULD SEE THAT— COULD
SEE HOW MY TRUE SELF
HAD DISAPPEARED—

SHE COULD SEE THAT I COULDN'T HELP MYSELF,

AND SHE COULD SEE THAT SHE COULDN'T HELP ME EITHER.

NOT IN THE WAY I NEEDED.

BUT SHE KNEW WHAT COULD.

AND I'm GLAD I FINALLY LISTENED.

CHAPTER NINE

GRADUATING... MAYBE?

PROUD THERAPY GRADUATE!

CLASS OF '05... and '07... and '11... and '14... and...

AT SOME POINT, YOU MIGHT FIND YOURSELF FEELING CONSISTENTLY BETTER. MAYBE YOU MISS A SESSION OR TWO WITHOUT NOTICING ANY NEGATIVE EFFECTS.

MAYBE YOU FEEL STABLE! RESILIENT! Happy, EVEN!

MAYBE YOU START TO WONDER IF IT'S TIME TO STEP away FROM THERAPY.

IT FEELS good WHEN all your HARD WORK payS OFF!

BUT aRE you READY To graduate?

IT CAN BE JUST aS SCARY aND NERVE-WRACKING TO STOP THERAPY aS IT IS TO START! BUT IT'S EMPOWERING TO PUT all THE LESSONS OF THERAPY INTO PRACTICE IN YOUR DaILY LIFE...

AND gRaDuaTing DOESN'T always MEAN BEING DONE FOREVER.

REMEMBER, THERAPY IS JUST ANOTHER TOOL FOR EMOTIONAL SELF-CARE, ANOTHER WAY TO FEEL BETTER AND WHETHER IT'S YOUR FIRST TIME GOING OR YOUR FIFTH TIME GOING BACK, IT'S ALWAYS THERE FOR YOU. ♡

SIGNS THERAPY IS WORKING

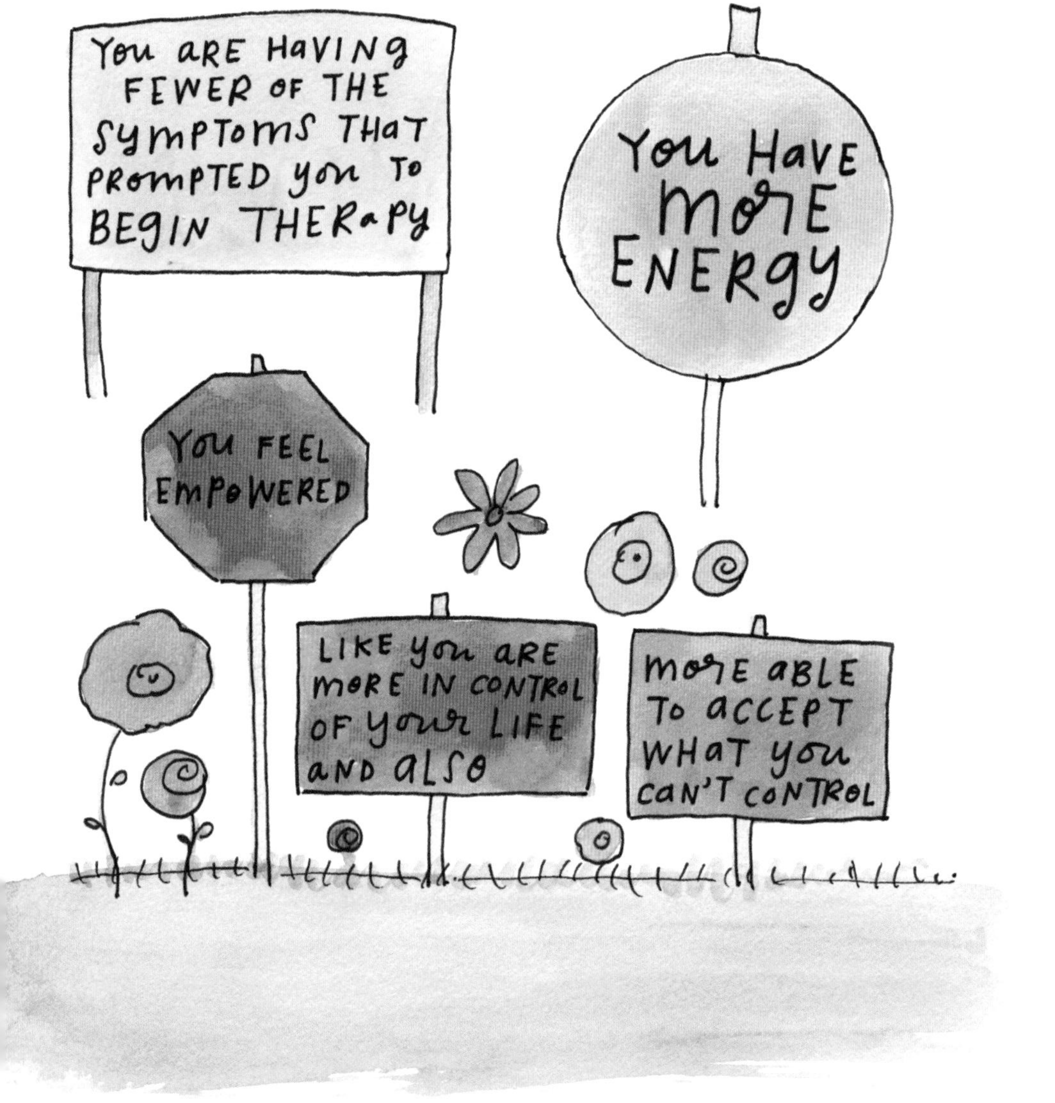

YOU ARE PUTTING THE SKILLS you LEARNED IN THERAPY INTO Day-To-Day PRACTICE

You aRE TaKINg BETTER CaRE OF youRSELF

THE PEOPLE CLOSEST TO you NOTICE you'VE CHANGED

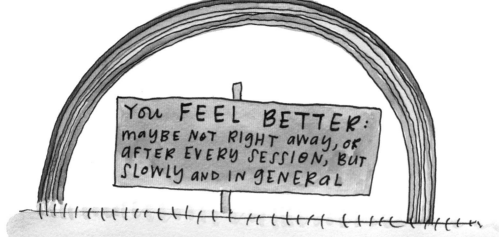

You FEEL BETTER: MAYBE NOT RIGHT AwAY, OR AFTER EVERY SESSION, BUT SLOWLY AND IN GENERAL

WEEKLY THERAPY CHECK-IN ♥

WEEK OF: _____

THIS WEEK I FELT:

☐ TURBULENT ☐ CALM ☐ IN-BETWEEN
☐ SAD ☐ ANGRY ☐ HAPPY ☐ TIRED
☐ ENERGIZED ☐ TENDER ☐ ABSENT
☐ CAPABLE ☐ OVERWHELMED
☐ _____ ☐ _____
☐ _____ ☐ _____
☐ _____ ☐ _____

BEFORE MY THERAPY SESSION, I FELT:

_____
_____
_____
_____
_____

AFTER MY SESSION, I FELT: _____

_____

_____

_____

_____

_____

SOMETHING I'm glAD WE TALKED
ABOUT IS: _____

_____

_____

_____

_____

SOMETHING I'D LIKE TO WORK ON
THIS WEEK IS: _____

_____

_____

_____

_____

_____

HOW TO STEP BACK FROM THERAPY

Talk to your THERAPIST FIRST. LET THEM KNOW you are CONSIDERING a CHANGE. THEY'LL BE glad TO gIVE you INPUT and PERSPECTIVE, and THEY'LL WORK WITH you TO come up WITH a PLAN you're COMFORTABLE WITH.

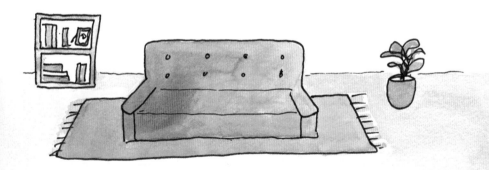

BRUSH UP ON YOUR SELF-CARE SKILLS.

MAKE SURE YOU HAVE THE TOOLS YOU NEED TO SUPPORT YOUR MENTAL HEALTH OUTSIDE OF THERAPY, FOR WHEN DIFFICULT TIMES INEVITABLY ARISE.

SELF-
CARE ♥
PLAN

TRY SPACING OUT YOUR SESSIONS.

IF YOU'RE NOT SURE YOU ARE QUITE READY TO QUIT OUTRIGHT, TRY PUTTING MORE TIME BETWEEN SESSIONS AND SEE HOW YOU FEEL.

JULY
M T W TH F Sa Su

MONITOR your mood.

PAY ATTENTION TO HOW you FEEL DAY TO DAY. NOTICE IF you SEEM TO BE HAVING MANY BAD DAYS IN a ROW... MAYBE IT'S TIME TO CHECK IN WITH your THERAPIST FOR a TUNE-UP?

LET SOMEONE KNOW.

ASK a LOVED ONE FOR HELP AS you TRANSITION OUT OF THERAPY. MAYBE THEY CAN HELP you MONITOR your FEELINGS, OFFER you SUPPORT AND ENCOURAGEMENT, OR LEND a LISTENING EAR.

DON'T CUT TIES.

MAKE AN AGREEMENT WITH YOUR THERAPIST TO KEEP IN TOUCH IN WHATEVER WAY WORKS BEST FOR YOU BOTH, SO YOU CAN BE SURE TO...

KEEP THE DOOR OPEN. ♡

REMEMBER— THERAPY IS AN ACT OF SELF-CARE, AND IT'S ONE YOU CAN RETURN TO IF YOU NEED IT.

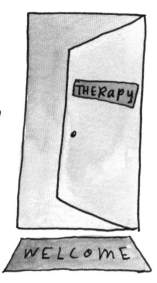

THERAPY IS THERE FOR YOU

IT FEELS GOOD TO **FEEL BETTER.** ♥

AND IT FEELS ESPECIALLY GOOD TO FEEL **BETTER ENOUGH** TO GRADUATE FROM THERAPY. ✳

BUT REMEMBER: GRADUATING DOESN'T MEAN YOU WILL FEEL BETTER FOREVER. ✳

HUMANS AREN'T STATIC.

HUMAN LIVES AREN'T STATIC.

WE ALL GROW AND CHANGE AND ENCOUNTER NEW CHALLENGES. WE MAKE NEW DECISIONS, WE EXPERIENCE NEW Traumas.

WHICH IS WHY I THINK OF
THERAPY as a PRACTICE:
a TOOL RATHER THAN a CURE
a RESOURCE
RATHER THAN a SOLUTION

SOMETIMES you'll Sail along in
LIFE WITH VERY LITTLE EFFORT

OTHER TIMES you'll NEED To LEAN
HEAVILY ON your PRACTICES OF
EMOTIONAL SELF-CARE To get By.

AND STILL OTHER TIMES,
EVEN ALL OF THOSE may NOT
BE QUITE ENOUGH.

IN THOSE TIMES, REMEMBER
THERAPY IS always
THERE FOR you: a SPACE
OF SAFETY AND COMFORT,
NURTURING AND growth.

AND you CAN
NEVER graduate
FROM growing.

RESOURCES

For IMMEDIaTE HELP IF you are IN CRISIS

♡ NaTIONaL SUICIDE PREVENTION LIFELINE: (800) 273-8255
SUICIDEPREVENTIONLIFELINE.ORG

For AFFORDaBLE THERaPY

♡ OPENPaTHCOLLECTIVE.ORG:
PROFESSIONaL THERaPISTS aT a
REDUCED COST, $30-$60/SESSION

♡ TaLKSPaCE.com, BETTERHELP.com:
ONLINE THERaPY WITH LICENSED
THERaPISTS & REaSONaBLE RaTES

For FINDING a THERaPIST

♡ PSYCHOLOGYTODAY.com:
A MASSIVE DATABASE OF
THERAPISTS, SEARCHABLE BY
LOCATION, PRACTICE STYLE,
ISSUES TREATED, GENDER,
SPIRITUAL BELIEFS, & MORE

♡ CHECK WITH your HEALTH
INSURANCE, CAMPUS HEALTH
CENTER, OR EAP(EMPLOYEE
ASSISTANCE PROGRAM)

♡ CONTACT a MENTAL HEALTH ORG
FOR GUIDANCE:

· NATIONAL ASSOCIATION OF SOCIAL
WORKERS: HELPSTARTSHERE.ORG

· NATIONAL ALLIANCE ON MENTAL
HEALTH: NAMI.ORG

· FINDTREATMENT.SAMHSA.GOV

THANK YOU

THIS BOOK WOULD NOT EXIST WITHOUT:

DAVID, CLAIRE, & LUCY, LIGHTS OF MY LIFE

MARIAN LIZZI, my magical EDITOR

DR. KRISTEN BRENDEL, PURVEYOR OF WISDOM AND INSIGHT AND A UNIVERSE OF ENCOURAGEMENT

RACHEL SUSSMAN, AGENT EXTRAORDINAIRE & GENERAL LIGHT IN THE DARKNESS

EVERYONE WHO HAS SUPPORTED, RELATED TO, AND BELIEVED IN ME ♡

OF COURSE, MY THERAPIST. THANKS, J.

ABOUT THE AUTHOR

TORI PRESS IS AN ARTIST AND WRITER AND HIGHLY ANXIOUS HUMAN BEING.

A 20-YEAR VETERAN OF THE BENEFITS OF THERAPY, SHE USES HER ART TO HELP ERASE THE STIGMA THAT STOPPED HER FROM SEEKING HELP FOR SO LONG.

SHE LIVES IN LOS ANGELES WITH HER HUSBAND, TWO DAUGHTERS, AND WHATEVER HOUSEPLANTS SHE HASN'T KILLED YET.